THE SEE SERIES

PSALMS

A DEVOTIONAL COMMENTARY

CHRIS TIEGREEN

See your worship with new eyes

Visit Tyndale online at tyndale.com.

Visit Tyndale Momentum online at tyndalemomentum.com.

Tyndale, Tyndale's quill logo, *Tyndale Momentum*, and the Tyndale Momentum logo are registered trademarks of Tyndale House Ministries. Tyndale Momentum is a nonfiction imprint of Tyndale House Publishers, Carol Stream, Illinois.

Psalms: A Devotional Commentary: See Your Worship with New Eyes

Designed by Dean H. Renninger

Published in association with the literary agency of Mark Sweeney and Associates, Carol Stream, Illinois.

For information about special discounts for bulk purchases, please contact Tyndale House Publishers at csresponse@tyndale.com, or call 1-855-277-9400.

ISBN 978-1-4964-8541-0

Printed in India

31 30 29 28 27 26 25
7 6 5 4 3 2 1

For Hannah

Contents

The See Series

Human beings live by vision. We're directed by the images in our minds. We pursue goals when we can *see* them; we grow according to examples we've observed more than the knowledge we've learned; and we embrace hope, despair, and numerous other perspectives based on what we see happening around us. Even people who don't think of themselves as visionary tend to have some mental picture of where they are headed and why. It's the way we're wired.

Most of us have a big vision—a sense of ultimate meaning and destiny, or even just a dream or a goal for our lives. We want to live with purpose. We orient our lives by what we can picture.

We also have smaller visions—what's on the agenda for today, this week, this year, or even the next couple of decades—that shape our short-term decisions.

If our little visions and big vision don't align with each other, we feel frustrated and compromised, as if our lives are going nowhere and our desires may never be fulfilled. But if we can align these visions and see clearly, we grow steadily, even dramatically, into our purpose and calling.

SEE, BE, LIVE

Christian teaching hasn't always recognized our visionary nature. Much instruction over the years has been based on a know-it-then-do-it approach to Scripture—as if life change were simply a matter of learning the truth and applying it. But such an approach bypasses heart transformation and can easily become legalistic and frustrating.

Though knowing and doing are both very important, following Jesus is more than a matter of knowledge and willpower. We can never *will* ourselves to be who we need to be. We are not called simply to *do*; we are called to *be*. When we put knowing and doing before being, we end up in the same condition that many of the scribes and Pharisees of Jesus' time found themselves in—as pious people aiming to live godly lives without the necessary inner transformation.

Let me explain what I mean by *knowing*—an unfortunately imprecise word in English. We might read the Bible and *know* the commandments, instructions, encouragement, and truth it conveys. We receive that information and even agree with it. And if we want to be obedient, we will act on what we know. In that sense, our approach is both cognitive and behavioral—our thoughts affect our actions. But knowledge alone won't change our hearts, motives, desires, impulses, and everything else in us that needs to be transformed.

We see this phenomenon in the multitudes of people who memorize Jesus' words about faith but still lie awake all night with worry; who love Psalm 23 but still believe they are pursued by misfortune, not goodness and mercy; who agree that Jesus is Lord but don't live as though he is. Knowledge and action alone aren't comprehensive and compelling enough to reshape us.

In addition to our intellectual or informational knowledge, we also live from a particular worldview that shapes everything about us. This, too, is *knowing*, but it's a radically different kind of knowledge, isn't it? It's how we see the world, which is why I prefer words such as *seeing* and *vision* to capture it. This kind of knowledge goes well beyond information and instructions. It reflects not only *what* we know but also *how* we know and how we *respond* (perhaps even unconsciously) to what we know. It forms our sense of identity and becomes the filter for every piece of information we receive. Whereas the first kind of knowing may shape our *thoughts* to a degree, this kind shapes our *thought processes* (and therefore our thoughts) to a greater degree.

For example, if I dive into a lake or ocean and swim around for an hour or two, I experience something of marine life. I can practice different strokes, get used to holding my breath for longer periods, and work on distances and techniques. I *know* swimming. I might even start to think I swim like a fish. But if I'm a fish, moving around in the water is my nature. I don't even have to think about strokes or breath or what it takes to live in the water. I just do it. I know swimming without even knowing that I know it. It's part of who I am.

God has given us a new nature and called us to live from it. It's a radical transformation—so radical that we aren't quite sure how to do it. Many of us turn back to old paradigms, trying to live out our new life by reforming our old nature. We try to make the new ways "natural," often by disciplining ourselves to conform to what we believe is true. In other words, we *know* and *do* by receiving information and acting on it.

But what if we really saw ourselves as new creations and gave no thought to any other possibility? What if it never even occurred to us that God might not be working in all the circumstances of our lives? What if love and worship were the default settings of our lives and we were shocked by anything else that came out of our hearts? What if our new nature was . . . well, natural?

There is no flip of a switch that gets us there, but some ways are better than others. I've experienced the futility of self-discipline born of knowing and doing (which, again, though insufficient, are still important). But I've also experienced the transformation that comes from that second kind of knowing—the radical reorientation of a worldview that shapes everything about us.

I call this radical reorientation *seeing* because we often express this deeper, more comprehensive knowledge in visual terms.

"I know you told me this would work, but I didn't *see* how."

"I knew she cared, but now I *see* how much."

"You can argue with me all you want, but the way I *see* it . . ."

We instinctively know there's a seeing that goes deeper than informational knowledge, and this seeing transforms vital elements of our personality—our hopes and dreams; our gut feelings; our deeply rooted attitudes, instincts, and motives. Knowing information and responding to it may or may not change our heart. A radically new perspective does.

Embracing a new worldview may be catapulted forward by visual or sensory knowledge, or by seeing in a new way. They say a picture is worth a thousand words—a *million* seems closer to the mark—and is far more memorable. That's why the Bible is full of stories, parables, and experiences; why God inspired prophets to see visions and illustrate truth in tangible ways; and why he eventually clothed himself in human flesh to live among us. From beginning to end, God gives us images—highly visual and symbolic representations of who he is and what he does. We don't just read his instructions; we see what living out the truth looks like. We don't just read that he is a deliverer; we see numerous examples of dramatic deliverance. He doesn't just tell us he cares for us; he inspires a king to portray him as a shepherd and his Son to dramatize sacrificial, unconditional love in eternally indelible ways. Those pictures and portrayals are life-changing.

If how we live flows out of who we are, being must come before doing. And if *seeing* so profoundly shapes *being*, then having this life-changing vision is vital. It is the key to the transformation we long for—that is, we become what we behold. The Holy Spirit works powerfully on the screens of our minds. We are drawn to whatever we focus on and emulate what we admire. Discipleship that begins with vision flows much more naturally into being and doing. Vision stirs us to be who we're called to be and to live as we're called to live.

The significance of our vision is the premise behind this devotional commentary series. The goal is to embrace a holistic, visual mode of learning. This series assumes that because we, as human beings, live from our identity and follow whatever vision we have, transformation happens by seeing in new ways. Instead of encouraging us simply to *know* and then *do*, the aim of these commentaries is to cast a vision for us to *see*, then *be*, then *live*. Like Jesus, who incorporated visual language into all his teaching, this series aims to refocus our inner eye. If we can see what the biblical writers saw and live according to that vision, we can be transformed.

THE ART OF ENVISIONING

We must train our brains to see and think in new ways. It doesn't just happen. The biblical mandate to renew our minds implies a conscious reorientation of our thought life. Old thought patterns are stubborn; those established neural pathways actively resist new pathways as intruders (which is why New Year's resolutions, exercise and diet plans, and quitting a bad habit can be so difficult). In most areas of life, this neurological dynamic—tapping into our established neural pathways—is helpful; we don't have to relearn everything each day. But when we've been called to reorient the way we think, we have to be relentless about it.

At a practical level, we can greatly amplify this process by (1) recognizing the vision behind biblical texts; (2) immersing ourselves in that vision (declaring the truths of Scripture out loud can help with this, as our brain is very responsive to the sound of our own voice, even if, at first, we don't think we sound convincing); and (3) practicing the art of envisioning.

This latter practice has been somewhat disparaged over the past couple of centuries because we've associated it with "imagination"—as in, "that's *only* your imagination," or "that's just a figment of your imagination," as if our internal vision is no reflection of reality. This would be news to biblical prophets, psalmists, storytellers, and teachers of parables, who all used highly visual language to express truth. Our imagination *can* be used to disengage us from reality—in fact, that's what many people do with it—but it is also our primary means of envisioning truth, which is exactly why God gave us so many stories and images and illustrations. He *wants* us to see his Kingdom—to picture his nature, his purposes, and his work in our lives. It's impossible to read Jesus' parables, study the stories in Acts or in the Old Testament historical books, or read the Psalms and Prophets without developing certain images in our minds. Our lives change when we immerse ourselves in those images.

In envisioning the Kingdom of God and all God's ways, we aren't trying to convince ourselves of something that *isn't* true—simply a figment of our imagination. We're training ourselves in what *is*. Sanctified imagination is not a flight from reality; it's a flight directly into it. We insist that our natural minds, long steeped in limited vision and distorted ways of thinking, must now conform to reality as God defines it.

That's when transformation occurs. When we see God, ourselves, our world, and his Kingdom as he does, we rarely have to discipline ourselves to live differently. We just do it.

IN THIS COMMENTARY

Because this is a *devotional commentary*, you will find material here that fits both descriptors: commentary on the text, and devotional or inspirational thoughts that apply the text to your life, specifically in the ways you see, become transformed, and live out that transformation. In this commentary, you will find

- an introduction to the biblical book;
- an introduction for each subsection of the book, explaining its place and purpose in the text, the context or background of that section, and how it fits into the big-picture vision of biblical truth;
- a series of devotionals on the text that
    - further explain context, background, meaning, and purpose,
    - offer suggestions for practical application,
    - inspire and challenge you to *re-envision*—to learn to see in new ways;
- a discussion guide in the back to help you further reflect on the Scripture passages and talk about them with others to expand your spiritual vision even more.

As you read, practice the art of envisioning. Pray for Holy Spirit–inspired perspectives. Notice what and how the biblical writers see, and immerse your heart and mind in those visions. Adopt them as your own. More and more, you will enter into the heights and depths of God's Kingdom and live in his ways.

INTRODUCTION TO PSALMS

Ancient Israelites lived in a world full of gods. These gods varied from region to region, and their images took on various animal and humanlike forms. The mythology surrounding them was diverse—so were their characteristics and abilities. But human responses to these deities generally involved bowing before them, making sacrifices and offerings to them (primarily to remain in their good graces), performing various rituals, seeking their favor, and uttering blessings, curses, and incantations in their names. Many of those responses were relatively benign. Others involved sexual immorality and death.

As much as we'd like to think God's people consistently separated themselves from these influences, many of them did not. Scripture describes how some erected shrines and altars to deities other than Yahweh (the personal name of God as revealed to the people of Israel). Even those who worshiped Yahweh exclusively did so in a context of established cultic practices. Israel's definitions of worship were often shaped by ancient understandings of diverse pantheons.

But God had called his people to be holy—set apart, distinct from the nations around them—and he made it clear that he alone was to be worshiped. The Psalms major on this theme and repeatedly turn Israel's worship toward the only true God, the Most High. Many psalmists were vying for pure worship of Yahweh not only among surrounding nations but also among their own people. Much of what we read in this worship collection comes from a felt need to emphatically declare the glories of Yahweh above all.

The idea that this God actually cared about how someone thought and behaved—notice how deeply personal many of the psalms are, compared to other sections of Scripture—made Israel's faith downright revolutionary. Most pagan gods were seen as wanting only to be ritually appeased and flattered, caring little for morality and ethics. In this religious context, the Psalms stood out with their emphasis on a personal relationship with the one true God.

Ancient Israelites before Solomon's reign, and sometimes after, also lived in a world that saw Israel as an upstart kingdom, a people who perhaps should not be a people (or at least should not have the influence or land that they had). The period of the kingdom's birth and infancy was not easy. Adversaries abounded. The ancient Near East was a cutthroat world, and in any time of weakness, enemies were waiting to take advantage. For this reason, themes of protection, provision, shelter, and vindication are woven throughout the Psalter. God's people called on him as their Rock and Deliverer, their Shepherd and Warrior, their Helper in times of need.

The Psalms were written *as* worship (the writing being an act of worship in itself) and *for* worship (to be used by individuals and the community). The Hebrew word for this worship collection is *Tehillim*, meaning "praises." Even laments and complaints in the Psalms ultimately point toward praise, the whole point being to live the entirety of our lives—even at their messiest and ugliest places—in God's presence.

The compilation of psalms in their current form seems to have taken place in the Second Temple era, after God's people had returned from the Babylonian captivity to rebuild Jerusalem and the Temple (post-538 BC). For that reason, the order and organization of the Psalms serve the needs and interests of worshipers in that period. But many were clearly written much earlier than that. Many come from David's time (and from David himself), and one is attributed to Moses. But even early psalms carry messages that resounded centuries later—leading up to the Babylonian captivity, during it, and in the time of restoration. About four centuries passed between the time of David and the Captivity, and the people of Israel (or Israel and Judah, once they split into northern and southern kingdoms) experienced the full scope of life and worship in those years.

Some psalms may have originated for no other reason than the creative expression of the worshiper. Others were written specifically for congregational use (as seen in 1 Chronicles 16:7 and psalms designated "for the choir director"). Since few give us clues about their historical context, by design they apply to the entire range of human experiences. Regardless of their origins, the Psalms have always resonated with God's people in the wide range of experiences they have faced.

The Psalms are full of images. For example, David didn't just tell us that God takes care of him; he pictured God as his Shepherd who led him to green pastures and quiet streams. The Psalms are exercises in envisioning because the psalmists needed visions to cling to. They saw God as their Rock, hid in the shelter of his wings, pictured his throne above dark clouds, and saw themselves as deep-rooted trees or deer panting for God's presence. Comforting words would have been reassuring, but images stick with us through painful, disorienting times. They have the power to dramatically change our perspective.

That's why the Psalms have been richly treasured by so many people over the centuries. They have long played a central role in Jewish, Orthodox, Catholic, and Protestant worship. The New Testament tells us that Jesus sang hymns (likely psalms; see Matthew 26:30) and urges us to do so too (Colossians 3:16; see also James 5:13). In our moments of both deepest distress and highest praise, they center our lives in the glories of God.

LIFE AS AN ANCIENT ISRAELITE

If you were an Israelite during the time of David or Solomon, you might have been gratified that an established monarchy was making your nation like others (see 1 Samuel 8:5, 19-20), but you would also be aware of its precarious position surrounded by much larger kingdoms. Yes, it was still the Promised Land, and you would see your piece of it as your family's divine inheritance. But other nations might not see it that way. Was that inheritance really safe?

You would sometimes hear the taunts of your enemies—from Canaanites still within the kingdom, or from other nations beyond it. Those taunts might be anti-Israel or anti-Yahweh or both—as in, "Where is your God?" (Psalm 42:3; 79:10; 115:2). You might cry out to God for protection or justice, whether on your own or as a nation (26:1; 43:1; 44:26; see also 135:14) and ask God to vindicate you and glorify his name (79:9). These were bold statements of faith. You'd be aware that the worship of Yahweh was central—David made that clear—but also that hidden away in many areas of the kingdom (and sometimes not so hidden away; see 1 Samuel 19:11-13) were altars and images of other gods. Declaring dependence on Yahweh and praising him above all were claims that stood out in a religiously diverse culture.

If you were an Israelite in the centuries after Solomon, the kingdom may have, at times, felt more established, but worship of Yahweh was still a point of contention. There were also times, as in the days of Elijah and Elisha, that Baal was more widely honored than Israel's God. Small, rival nations periodically posed problems, and larger empires still loomed over the horizon. And as prophets warned, judgment was coming. Assyria sacked the northern kingdom of Israel in 722 BC. Babylon invaded Jerusalem in 597 BC and destroyed the city and the Temple in 586 BC. These were precarious times too.

If you were an exile returning from Babylonian or Persian lands after the Captivity ended, you would have a different outlook—not one of establishing a kingdom where you were, but rather one of rebuilding a society from scratch. Your people would still be under Persian rule, your neighbors would treat you as intruders, and you'd wonder if Jerusalem and its Temple could ever be restored to their former glory. But you'd also know that God had once accomplished a miraculous exodus for his people and placed them in a Promised Land after driving out hostile people. You'd long for him to do it again. And in light of his past promises, lost hopes would be resurrected.

Psalms were written, compiled, and used in worship in all these contexts, and it's best that they don't always tell us which one. What comes down to us is a collection of familiar human experiences lived under the watchful eye of the God who cares about them all—our longings, pains, fears, victories, defeats, joys, griefs, guilt, shame, and hopes for now and forever. When we freely express these to God and invite him into the experience, he shows up—just as he did long ago. He redirects our focus, stretches and strengthens our faith, and opens our hearts more and more to who he is so we can experience him in deeper ways. The Psalms are a veritable training manual in how to see with spiritual eyes and live life fully in God's presence.

THE LITERATURE OF PSALMS

We don't know who authored many of the psalms. We can be sure that many were written by David, although we might wonder if all attributed to him were by him. "Of David," broadly understood, can mean by him, about him, for him, in his honor, or in his tradition. The same is true for psalms of Asaph or any other named person. Some psalms of David speak of the king in the third person, suggesting they were written about him (though it's possible he referred to himself that way). Because the attributions were likely not in the original text, and because these attributions can have multiple meanings, the following devotionals and commentary will sometimes refer to the author simply as "the psalmist" to cover all the possibilities. Regardless of who wrote them, they are versatile enough to apply to a wide range of experiences, both in the reigns of kings and in the faith of everyday people throughout history.

The Psalms are written in a variety of genres and forms, and they focus on a variety of topics. In terms of genre, they can be individual or communal laments, hymns of praise, thanksgiving psalms, royal psalms, Torah or wisdom psalms, and processionals, among other genres. Thematically, they can include messianic themes and prophecies, complaints, curses, celebrations of the king's enthronement, and much more. Structurally, some are acrostics (in which each line, verse, or stanza begins with a successive letter of the Hebrew alphabet), and many are organized into groupings that share a common purpose.* The collection as a whole is divided into five books, each with a somewhat distinctive outlook, though connecting with overarching themes throughout. Many of these genres, forms, and themes will be introduced throughout this book.

* You may have come across different numberings for the Psalms. The Hebrew Old Testament and the Greek translation of it (the Septuagint) differ. Orthodox traditions follow the Greek version; most Protestant Bibles (and this devotional commentary) follow the Hebrew numbering.

Most of the key themes will be explored further in the following pages, but some of the major ones can be summarized as follows:

- Several psalms, including the first, extol the **Torah** and call God's people to delight in his instruction. The righteous (who love the law) and the wicked (who ignore it) are on different paths, and those paths lead to very different outcomes.
- **Kingship** is a repeated theme throughout the book, as we will see in several royal psalms. The backdrop to most of these is the Davidic covenant—God's promise to establish David's throne forever—and some of these psalms foreshadow a messianic ruler. The Psalms embrace both human and divine kingship, with the two sometimes merged into one. From a Christian perspective, Jesus is both the exemplar and the fulfiller of many royal psalms.
- Many psalms recall **redemptive history**, particularly the exodus from Egypt, but also with an eye to a second exodus, from captivity in Babylon. God's great works in delivering his people from Egypt into the Promised Land were landmark events in Israel's history.
- Many of God's promises to Israel involved **land and inheritance**. Each covenant in Israel's history, from Abraham's calling to the establishment of David's everlasting kingdom, was land-based. There's a marvelous ambiguity in the Hebrew word for "land," which can also mean "earth." While the Israelites often understood God's promises to apply to the specific land—its abundance, fruitfulness, renewal, and kingdom character—we can see them applying to the entire earth as well.
- The Psalms reveal many facets of **God's nature** and call him by many names. He is the Creator, Redeemer, Rescuer, Rock, Shepherd, Fortress, and much more. These not only tell us who God is but more specifically who he is *for us*—practically. God is not content just to describe himself. He shows his people who he is through their experiences.

- Several psalms focus on **creation**—the majesty and glory of God's works, his self-revelation through what he has made. God brings order out of chaos and beauty out of brokenness. If he has created so miraculously, he can re-create miraculously too—a profound comfort to any reader of the Psalms who is in need of renewal and restoration.
- ***Shalom*** is a Hebrew term that is hard to translate but involves the fullness, wholeness, completeness, satisfaction, and peace of life with God. Included in that concept are many personal blessings but also a just and righteous society. Many psalms calling for shalom (usually translated "peace") therefore emphasize justice, relief for the poor, and defense of the helpless.
- Many psalms begin in deep need and end with fulfillment, or at least hopes for it. This interplay between **need and fulfillment** demonstrates God's presence and power in the lives of his people. He answers the cries of the human heart and meets us in our brokenness—spiritually and practically.
- Some psalmists discover who they are as they pour out their hearts to God. As we read the Psalms, our vision of our **identity** is reoriented; we come to see ourselves as his people crowned with glory and honor, his sheep, the delight of his eyes, his intricate creations who are fearfully and wonderfully made. As the psalmists demonstrate, God often shifts our perceptions of who we are before he leads us to act or gives us his plan for our lives.
- Above all else, the Psalms demonstrate the **primacy of praise**. This is what we were created for and how we find our deepest, highest fulfillment.

The Psalms provide an occasion for us to immerse ourselves in God's presence and the nature of his Kingdom. We can read the Bible and listen to sermons all day long, but the truth that we read or hear just fades away after a few days, unless we are cultivating the Kingdom within us. The soil of our hearts needs to be right. Otherwise the seeds never grow; or they grow for a little while and then wither and die (Matthew 13:1-23). This is why Paul urged his readers to sing psalms; it's one way to stir up a Kingdom environment within us (see Colossians 3:12-17). In many respects, this is what the Psalms are about. They are case studies in truth taking root in the heart, where God ultimately wants his Word and his Spirit to dwell.

BOOK 1: PSALMS 1–41

Ancient Israel was planted in a world that generally assumed subjection to the whims of capricious storm gods, fertility goddesses, and a multitude of other deities that might—but might not—harness the forces of nature for mere humans. Early psalmists (primarily David) were living at a time when Israel was being established as a kingdom, separating from ungodly influences around it (with mixed results). They were trying to subdue threats—both internal opposition from remaining Canaanites and external opposition from neighboring peoples like Philistia, Edom, Moab, Ammon, and Aram—and were experiencing conflict on several fronts. In their divinely ordained sense of identity, the people of Israel were not just members of any nation; they were God's people, and their kingdom was God's Kingdom on earth.

BACKGROUND

Most of the psalms in Book 1 are attributed to David, who reigned not long after the period of the judges, when everyone did what was right in their own eyes (Judges 21:25). Though God was establishing a human kingship over his people—at their request—and consolidating Israel as a kingdom embodying his rule, it was still very much a work in progress. Idolatry was widespread, and loyalties were split among rival kings (David's supporters at first against Saul's former supporters, then against competing movements like Absalom's). Some tribes were only loosely connected to Jerusalem, David's declared center of the kingdom. Dissent was common.

This context of power struggles, idolatry, and territorial disputes is evident in many of the psalms of Book 1. So are affirmations of God's supremacy, compassion, and help. Currents of confrontation flow through this book—at least one commentator sees this as its dominant theme.* As we read, we should see this conflict in terms of God's promises to David to establish his dynasty forever and to establish Mount Zion as God's dwelling place among his people. Attacks against David were not just personal affronts; they were attacks on God's purposes.

This dynamic in the Psalms portrays David as an "anointed one," a type of messiah (the Hebrew word from which we get *messiah* means "anointed one"). From a New Testament perspective, David points to the Messiah to come. He was at times extraordinarily merciful and at times violently opposed to those who violated God's purposes. Though he sometimes misdirected his passions, he was always zealous for God and his sanctuary. The anointed king was an anointed worshiper.

Was God ruling *over* David and Israel or ruling *with* David and Israel? This distinction is not clear in the Psalms; the divine and human thrones are often seen as in sync. In fact, this convergence of divine and human rule is an important development in Israel's history and worship. The beginning of the Psalter emphasizes David as king, and the end emphasizes God as King; but both are honored as king throughout.

---

* O. Palmer Robertson, *The Flow of the Psalms: Discovering Their Structure and Theology* (Phillipsburg, NJ: P&R Publishing, 2015), 52–53.

THE BIG PICTURE

The claims of the Davidic psalms are remarkable when we consider their context: an age in which Israel was trying to establish an earthly king and kingdom resembling the heavenly King and Kingdom—and doing so in the midst of pagan, idolatrous nations. It's quite a landmark statement in such a setting to say that God's love endures forever (lesser gods loved selectively, if they loved at all, and changed their minds often), or that Israel's God was above all gods (most nations honored deities that had power in their regions but not beyond). Ancient readers did not have centuries of theological creeds behind them to make these statements sound commonplace. These declarations were bold assertions of a reality different from what the world knew.

We need to recapture that sense of boldness and grasp how unique these declarations were. We don't live in the world of the psalmists, but our belief in Israel's God is increasingly challenged in our time. Like the psalmists, we make choices about which king and kingdom we will honor and which source of help we will depend on. The times have changed, but the ways of a fallen world have not. In the crucible of life, we call out to God just as the psalmists did.

You'll probably never fight any Philistines or try to survive a coup; but you will face challenges. You may be betrayed, go through an intense relational conflict, desperately pray for a loved one to turn to the Lord, suffer severe discouragement or depression, feel besieged by every situation and person around you, or simply struggle with daily life. Whatever hardships you find yourself facing, the psalms of this book are for you.

They are like trees planted along the riverbank, bearing fruit each season. Their leaves never wither, and they prosper in all they do.

1:3

The Psalms begin with a blessing. But this blessing doesn't apply to everyone who reads them; the joys it speaks of are given not to those who follow the ways of unrighteousness but to those who delight in God's instruction. In essence, Psalm 1 affirms God's law. It's a Torah psalm, a call to remember the covenant given at Mount Sinai, a promise that when our lives are aligned with God and his purposes, we will flourish. In other words, if you're looking for wholeness, fulfillment, fruitfulness, and joy—this is the key.

The central image for this psalm, a tree planted by a stream, sets the stage for all that is to come in orienting readers to God's purposes. This tree is deeply rooted in the land of promise, drawing from the refreshing flow of God's resources. It may have to weather storms, but it doesn't strive to achieve or overcome; trees don't search for their nourishment but rest in the nourishment of their environment. Neither does it grow impatient. A strong, productive tree will bear fruit in season. It simply lives, grows, and thrives.

RE-ENVISION YOUR ROOTS

Believe it or not, that's your calling—to live, grow, and thrive—and your self-perception is vital to it. Wherever you go, whatever you experience, however far your journey takes you, envision yourself as a flourishing tree. Choose God's truth daily, root yourself in his promises always, and draw from his Spirit constantly. You will take on his good, faithful, loving, true character. Trees are always shaped by their environment, and with good soil and proper nourishment, they grow increasingly stable, fruitful, and strong. You'll need to be patient for the seasons of life to unfold—a genuine challenge in a world addicted to instant gratification—but they will. And in one way or another, as the psalmist assures, you will prosper in all of them.

PSALM 2: THE SON'S (AND YOUR) INHERITANCE

Only ask, and I will give you the nations as your inheritance, the whole earth as your possession.

2:8

Psalm 1 emphasized God's word. Psalm 2 points to the Word made flesh, the Messiah. Whereas the first psalm spoke of personal flourishing, the second psalm speaks of geopolitics—the Kingdom of God and, more importantly, the King himself. He is so far above the nations, so unthreatened by the raging and scheming of human powermongers, that he laughs. He knows the end of every story, and neither he nor his people come out as losers in any of them. In fact, all the futility of human devices ultimately serves his purposes.

At the center of this Kingdom is the Son who reigns. He has been placed on the holy mountain, the spiritual apex of creation, to administer God's justice and inherit the nations as his own. All he has to do is ask. The earliest readers likely read the psalm in light of their current king. Over time, messianic interpretations developed and then were seen in an entirely new light by New Testament writers. But the unfolding layers of meaning add to the beauty of Scripture. As early Christians understood from this psalm, the raging, rebelling kingdoms of earth will be subdued and brought into the realm of God's Kingdom (Acts 4:24-28).

This psalm invites us to take refuge in the Son, the ultimate King of creation. But the New Testament invites us to do something more. We have been adopted into the royal family and have become co-heirs with this King (Romans 8:15-17; Ephesians 1:5, 11; 1 Peter 2:9). We are destined to rule and reign with him (2 Timothy 2:11-12; Revelation 1:6; 5:10; see also Ephesians 1:19-22; 2:6). We stand to inherit all that he inherits—that is, everything (see Colossians 1:16). No wonder those who take refuge in him are blessed.

RE-ENVISION YOUR INHERITANCE

Many Christians have filled their vision with "lost-cause" theology—a view that the church will continue to decline until its King returns to rescue it. But according to this psalm and Scripture as a whole, we are losing no battles, regardless of appearances. We were created, redeemed, and restored to have visions of victory. If our King is invited to ask for the nations and we are blessed to inherit all that he inherits, we can ask for them too—that he would draw them all into his glorious reign. Only with such bold requests can we fulfill our God-given mission in this world.

PSALM 3: A SHIELD AROUND YOU

You, O Lord, are a shield around me; you are my glory, the one who holds my head high.

3:3

God's promises were at stake. David had been promised a house in turmoil (2 Samuel 12:11-12)—his son's attempt at a violent coup certainly qualified—but he had also been promised an everlasting kingdom (2 Samuel 7:16). Although Absalom was an heir, he was surely not the heir God had in mind. (There's a profound difference between a son with the same DNA and a son with the same heart for God.) In fact, Absalom's attacks on David would have thwarted the promise by defeating God's anointed king—something David had steadfastly refused to do against his unworthy predecessor, Saul. So David cried out not only for his own deliverance but also for God's purposes.

This is one of many psalms that begins in crisis and ends in peace; and as in most cases, the circumstances have not changed from beginning to end. The only catalyst for change is David's plea—he cried out, and God heard him. He began by focusing on his thousands of enemies and shifted his focus to God as his glory and shield. The "ten thousand" (v. 6) were still there, but fear had gone. A situation that had once appeared as life-threatening danger now seemed safe, and David slept in peace.

That's what happens when we truly, deeply believe God's promises. Though David was experiencing God's chastisement for his sins, he knew the larger promise of an everlasting kingdom would not be compromised. Most of all, he was sure of God's salvation and blessing.

RE-ENVISION YOUR CRISIS

In the midst of a crisis, you have a choice: You can focus on problems and adversaries, or you can fix your eyes on God. One option leads to fear; the other to faith, peace, and rest—even before the situation changes. Victory does indeed come from the Lord (Psalm 3:8), but only the heart that sees it in advance can lie down and get up in peace (Psalm 4:8).

PSALM 4: YOUR PUBLIC DEFENDER

In peace I will lie down and sleep, for you alone, O LORD, will keep me safe.

4:8

David, the messianic figure from whose lineage the Messiah would one day come, was being maligned. He knew God as the one who declared him innocent (v. 1), but others were declaring quite the opposite. As seen with regard to the prophets, apostles, and especially Jesus, the testimony of human observers was often wrong. God's response in all these situations, including with David, was to vindicate his people—and, in the case of Jesus, to exalt him forever. This is how he handles attacks on his people.

David asked, "How long?" (v. 2), and the answer doesn't come in this psalm—and it often doesn't in our lives either. But David was thoroughly convinced of two things: God had set the godly apart for himself, and God would answer when he called (v. 3). The attacks on him were temporary. The vindication would endure forever.

RE-ENVISION YOUR REPUTATION

Far too many people measure themselves by other people's opinions. They see themselves through the eyes of their critics. God insists that we see ourselves through his eyes—as his holy ones, the object of his delight. When we take on his vision, we feel no compulsion to become defensive, push back, or lash out.

When we don't take on his vision, we think our lives are being destroyed by poisonous tongues.

They aren't, of course. God is your defender, your advocate, the guardian of your reputation, and the source of your joy. If you see your life being preserved by the God of perfect timing who reveals the truth and defends his people, you can be patient and strong while storms rage around (and at) you. One of the hardest things to do is remain secure and steadfast in your own cause while it's being maligned or you're being slandered. Yet sooner or later, God comes to the defense of his people. Look to him as your vindication and at yourself as his beloved, and rest in the safety of his care.

PSALM 5: A DEEPER NEED

Because of your unfailing love, I can enter your house; I will worship at your Temple with deepest awe.

5:7

David needed God's help—again—to the point that each day began with groaning. But each day also began with expectant prayer, which is not the same as desperate, hopeless, anxious prayer. In keeping with the themes of Psalm 1, the righteous (and, specifically, David) are contrasted with the wicked and the proud—those who lie and murder. But the righteous are not defined here as those without sin, only as those who take refuge in the Lord and love his name (v. 11). They will sing praises and be filled with joy—a far cry from the groaning that began this psalm.

Once again the path from desperate need to songs of joy is not a change in circumstances but a change in perspective. David knew he could enter God's presence not because of his own righteousness but "because of [God's] unfailing love." He was convinced he would worship at the Temple—quite a statement of faith, since the Temple was only a dream in David's heart at this point—and be awed by God's nature. Being in his presence is enough to radically change the way we see whatever we're going through.

RE-ENVISION YOUR NEED

You may be experiencing gaping needs or be recovering from deep wounds and wake up each morning with a heart that groans in search of divine help. Those needs are genuine, and God intends to meet them. But you also have another need he intends to meet—the need for a radically new perspective on your situation. The problem isn't always the problem. Sometimes your view of the problem is a much bigger issue.

Encountering God can change the way we see *everything*. When awe of him overwhelms us, nothing else does. When we magnify his name, our vision of him expands, our problems shrink, our faith rises, and our hearts are prepared to receive the answers he wants to bring.

PSALM 6: SEEING BEYOND THE PAIN

My vision is blurred by grief; my eyes are worn out because of all my enemies.

6:7

Psalm 6 is full of the fallen human condition with its distress, futility, guilt, and the prospect of judgment and death. There's outward oppression (from enemies) and inward pain (deep in the bones). Tears flow; visions of victory and vindication so common in surrounding passages are absent in this one. In fact, vision of any kind is hard to come by. It's "blurred by grief." Life in a fallen world tends to have that effect. We can't see clearly when we're focused on our pain.

In the previous psalm and the next one, David's enemies are guilty. In this one, he is. He knows that, and having already affirmed the fate of the unrighteous elsewhere, he knows the implications for himself. But he also knows something the wicked don't: God is a merciful healer and restorer. Even in despair, he can see God's unfailing love.

RE-ENVISION YOUR HOPES

Though the first seven verses of this psalm are brutal—seemingly hopeless, saturated with the grief, frustration, and pain of the human experience—the last two verses tell a completely different story. David goes from "when?" and "how long?" and "how much?" to a firm belief that God has heard and answered, even though the answer hasn't shown up yet. A core belief, a vision of who God is, has again made all the difference.

That vision of God is subtly evident in David's hope for restoration (v. 3). He assumes mercy and sees God as the restorer even of the guilt-ridden. Unlike those who suppose that this side of heaven is all about suffering, David believes he will see God's goodness in the land of the living (27:13). Even when he can't see clearly, he expects favor and blessing sooner or later.

That's what happens when faith settles into our hearts. We begin to see again. We experience an inward shift that so often precedes the outward shift we're hoping for. And we experience the God of restoration whom our desperate souls have longed for.

PSALM 7: THE GOD ON YOUR SIDE

I come to you for protection, O LORD my God. . . . I will thank the LORD because he is just.

7:1, 17

C. S. Lewis observed that the ancient Hebraic perception of God as Judge was far different from the later Christian view. Ancient Israelites rejoiced in God's justice and asked for it because they saw themselves as the plaintiffs and hoped for "a resounding triumph with heavy damages." Hence the appeals in various psalms to "judge my case," "uphold my cause," "avenge me," and so on. Christians tend to fear God's judgment, seeing it in the context of a criminal case with ourselves in the dock, hoping for a pardon.* In the latter case, God is against the guilty. In the former, he is for the oppressed.

Both sides of justice are true, of course, but here he is not only the Judge who defends his people but he is also the King over the nations of the world. He can be called upon to stand against enemies, to "wake up" and bring justice (v. 6), to foil the plots of the wicked and trap them in their own snares (vv. 15-16). The unrepentant should fear his judgments, but his people should seek them out. He is the God who is on our side.

RE-ENVISION YOUR SUPPORT

Some will argue that God is not on our side; we're on his. We orient ourselves to him, not the other way around. Yet Scripture portrays him as our defender,

* C. S. Lewis, *Reflections on the Psalms* (San Francisco: HarperCollins, 2017), 12.

protector, advocate, and even "helper"—often with the same word used of Eve in Genesis 2:18 (Psalm 28:7; 54:4; 115:10-11; 121:1). David saw God on our side (Psalm 124:1-2), and Paul insisted that he is "for us" (Romans 8:31). God invites you to envision him as he describes himself—as the God who is there for you, your helper and protector, your defender and upholder. The King over the world is the King who fights for you in your small corner of it, eager to uphold your cause.

PSALM 8: A GODLIKE CROWN

Yet you made them only a little lower than God and crowned them with glory and honor.

8:5

In the midst of a series of psalms about intense conflict with enemies comes a fresh breath of awareness of God's majesty and the beautiful mysteries of his creation. Enemies are mentioned here, too, and as in the surrounding psalms, they are far beneath the power and judgments of God. But the psalmist's reflections go all the way back to Creation—the moon and stars; animals of the land, sky, and sea; and human beings made out of mere dust into the glorious image of God himself. The true King of earth's nations is also the King of all creation, majestic in all his works.

The New Testament uses this passage to affirm the uniqueness of Jesus (Hebrews 2:6-10), but it refers to much more than a messianic exception. All human beings are "crowned . . . with glory and honor" and are positioned just a little lower than God himself. (Traditionally, "God" has been rendered "angels" here, but literally it's "God.") We are pictured in partnership with him. Just as his majestic name fills the earth, so do his people, bearing the glory and honor he has given us.

RE-ENVISION YOUR HUMANITY

The disclaimer "I'm only human" casually laments our limitations, but there is nothing "only" about our humanness. That's a cramped vision, a statement of lowered expectations and resignation to futility. It vastly underestimates what God wants to do for, in, and through his people. As an image-bearer of God, you are crowned with glory and honor and filled with the promise of restoration—the ultimate goal of your redemption. You are not God, but you are godly, a bona fide sharer of the divine nature (2 Peter 1:4). To see yourself as anything less sentences you to a mundane, broken existence. To see yourself as he does transforms you as drastically as an earthbound caterpillar becomes a butterfly in flight. A true vision of humanness opens you up to a whole new world of the supernatural, wonderful, awesome power and presence of God.

ACROSTIC PSALMS

Ancient societies depended heavily on oral communication. Modern readers are used to having access to written material, but very few people did in the ancient world—only the literary elite, who in many cases were also the religious elite. Certainly Israel's religious leaders had access to biblical and liturgical texts, but not necessarily always at their fingertips. Ordinary, faithful people, many of whom were non- or semi-literate, remembered hymns and poems by their melodies (tunes are marvelous memory aids) or by some other means. One of those means was an acrostic—lines, verses, or stanzas that begin with each successive letter of the alphabet.

Several psalms are structured acrostically. The order of initial letters provided hints for anyone trying to remember what came next. Psalms that fit this category include 9–10, 25, 34, 37, 111, 112, 119, and 145. (Psalms 9 and 10 were originally one psalm, as the acrostic structure bridges the two; the Septuagint, a Greek translation of the Old Testament, combines these as Psalm 9, which begins its different numbering of psalms from the Hebrew text.)

This creative technique has several purposes, most obvious of which is making the psalms easier to remember and recite in their original language. This clearly suggests that some psalms were meant to be memorized, whether for personal use in times of need, didactic use in an educational setting, or liturgical use in corporate worship. For individual use, psalmists expected readers and hearers to meditate on their words. In communal settings, these internal cues helped a cantor lead the singing (or for psalms sung or recited by a congregation, helped everyone keep up with the flow). The human mind loves order and retains structured information far better than disorganized facts.

The acrostic technique also conveys a message of completeness in some psalms, particularly Psalm 119, a Torah psalm in which the letters of the alphabet are used to organize not single verses but full stanzas. A Torah student aware of this structure would get the impression that God's Word is comprehensive, the beginning and the end, the alpha and the omega (see Revelation 1:8; 22:13)—or, as we might say, the A to Z—of divine wisdom. The very structure preaches a sermon: This psalm and the Word itself apply to all of life.

The LORD is a shelter for the oppressed, a refuge in times of trouble. Those who know your name trust in you, for you, O LORD, do not abandon those who search for you.

9:9-10

Perhaps you've noticed a theme in these first few psalms—an ongoing conflict between God's people and their enemies, and more specifically between God's chosen king and those who oppose his reign. But more is going on here than an ancient struggle for regional power. If we expand our vision to take in the bigger picture, we'll see a cosmic conflict between God and a rebellious planet, the enmity that naturally occurs between those who choose his way and those who choose their own, and the trials and turmoil of establishing his Kingdom on earth through the unlikely people he has chosen. From Israel's perspective, these conflicts were about nationhood. From the perspective of salvation history, they are about so much more.

David stood at a strategic point in the midst of this greater conflict. Now, in an entirely different time and context, so do you. That conflict still rages, and God's people are still key players in its outcome, which has been unfolding over millennia and will culminate with the return of the King. You have certainly experienced the friction in your personal life, but you've also seen it on the world stage. Until the King comes, the earth shakes under the weight of its own rebellion.

RE-ENVISION THE BATTLEFIELD

The New Testament tells us that all creation will be shaken so that only the unshakable remains (Hebrews 12:25-29). Where do you fit in that picture? When the battle rages around you, do you engage or retreat? Stand firm or wilt away? Rise up in faith or shudder in fear? Those whose eyes are filled only with battle scenes tend to either attack or retreat, but those who focus on God as their refuge—who are full of praise and joy and who testify of his goodness, as the psalm says—can remain in the battle without being flustered by it. We can live in faith and remain at rest, even with turmoil swirling around us. A vision of the unshakable King makes us unshakable ourselves.

PSALM 10: IN SEARCH OF JUSTICE

O LORD, why do you stand so far away?

10:1

It's easy to look at the world around us and wonder why so much of it is in chaos. We see violence, abuse, deception, betrayal, selfishness, greed, manipulation, poverty, despair, and rampant oppression and injustice. It's also easy to speculate about God's sovereignty in such times. *Why doesn't he step in?* The condition of the world has led many to conclude he doesn't exist. Even those who do believe in him sometimes wonder if he's some sort of absentee Father.

Psalm 10, like so many other psalms and prophetic writings, views the apparent distance of God through the lens of injustice. The proud and wicked were exploiting the poor and helpless for their own gain, and God's people looked to him for his righteous judgments. Yet those judgments were slow to come. Why? Perhaps it's because God sometimes allows evil to run its course in order to more thoroughly undo it with his intervention. Or maybe he was looking to his people to demonstrate his character by being his instruments of deliverance. Regardless of the reason, God does not stand far away from his people or this world. As the last line of the psalm promises, he *will* bring justice and end the terror of evildoers.

RE-ENVISION THE RIGHTEOUS AGENDA

Perhaps you've looked to God for solutions, praying and seeking answers. Have you ever seen yourself as one of the solutions? It's one thing to know about his righteousness, but it's another to take it upon yourself and live it out for the benefit of those who need to see it. We cannot see ourselves simply as believers in God and followers of Jesus; we are more than that. We are divinely ordained justices of the peace, cultural ambassadors for heaven, and carriers of shalom who are working out the fullness of the Kingdom on earth.

The world has its own brand of justice. The heart behind it may be good, but the definitions and details are often twisted. God the Righteous Judge has filled this world with agents and ambassadors of his goodness, and he seeks to work through us, not stand at a distance. In his name, we step into the chaos and speak life and peace to all its victims.

I trust in the LORD for protection. So why do you say to me, "Fly like a bird to the mountains for safety!"

11:1

David knew what it was like to "fly like a bird to the mountains." He had spent years eluding Saul's efforts to kill him. Now as king, he perhaps saw the absurdity of the righteous fleeing from the unrighteous—a necessary tactic at times, but still an outrageous reversal of the divine order. A younger David recognized this absurdity when he went to the front lines and heard the taunts of a giant Philistine (1 Samuel 17:26). Now, with a clear vision of God in his temple—the heavenly one, since the earthly one had not yet been built—David had recaptured that holy indignation.

Of course, David recognized that his battles were not just Israel's; they were God's. Still, this psalm remains very focused on individual lives—"those whose hearts are right" (v. 2) and "every person on earth" under God's careful examination (v. 4). While God had aimed his arrows at the wicked in Psalm 7, here the wicked are aiming arrows at God's people (v. 2). Even in highly personal, small-arena battles, God would protect and defend. Even more, he would show his face to the virtuous.

RE-ENVISION GOD'S CLOSENESS

Some people call out to God to come all the way down from heaven to help them in their personal battles. Others see him and his angels right there next to them, with divine swords drawn. It's not hard to predict which type of people would have more faith; our mental pictures both reflect and reinforce what we believe. If you see him as the King over nations but not over individual lives, including yours, you'll either run from battles or rely on your own strategies, neither of which ends well. Gaze into the face of the God who loves justice, be strengthened in your just cause, and trust that you will be richly rewarded.

The faithful have vanished from the earth!

12:1

Elijah made the mistake of thinking he was alone—that he was the last of Israel's faithful prophets and servants of God. God showed him otherwise by promising to preserve seven thousand devoted worshipers and to give him a co-worker and future replacement (1 Kings 19:3-18). Here David makes the same alarmist claim, fearing that the righteous were disappearing rapidly and that God's Kingdom was in decline. He saw the injustices going on around him and wondered if anyone remained faithful to God's ways.

Many in our time express the same lament, but it isn't true. In the grand trajectory of redemptive history, God's Kingdom is never in decline (see Isaiah 9:7). It is always advancing. Sometimes Kingdom growth is hard to see, but it's always there. Remember, we have a choice in what we focus on. Often our focus is on the crises of faith around us rather than on God's Kingdom. Contrary to the view of many that the world is getting worse and worse, the eyes of faith see the Kingdom expanding more and more.

RE-ENVISION PROGRESS

Many people set their gaze on what God *isn't* doing. That's natural; most of us tend to see whatever is wrong and try to fix it. But choose instead to notice what God *is* doing. There are massive movements of Christian growth and worship around the world—organic, grassroots, Spirit-led awakenings with the power to transform society. More people claim the name of Jesus than ever before. People in closed countries are waking up to the reality of Jesus. Reports that neglect such advances and focus on what we lack will only stir up anxiety and bitterness. But a focus on progress stirs up faith. In a world that thrives on negative news, shifting your vision from one to the other will take practice and persistence. But it will always fill you with hope.

PSALM 13: CHOOSE TO SING

I will sing to the LORD because he is good to me.

13:6

This psalm certainly does not begin with a song of gratitude. It begins with a lament, a complaint, and a plea for deliverance and vindication. David is in a dire situation, endlessly stuck in anguish, it seems, under the thumb of his gloating enemies. For the anointed one of Israel, a king who was promised an everlasting kingdom, the incongruity had to be shocking and disorienting. How could God's king and kingdom be in such a position? Where was the crown of glory and honor he bestowed on his people (Psalm 8:5)? God's victorious king didn't seem very victorious.

God is content with such anomalies—for a time. He let righteous Joseph and Daniel serve pagan kings. He let prophets suffer at the hands of ungodly persecutors. He let the beloved Son, the Lord of the universe, be buried in a tomb. All were vindicated in time—gloriously so—but he seemed in no rush with some of them. The treasures of the Kingdom are often hidden in unsightly vessels and underneath disturbing circumstances. It's easy to get stuck in the middle of the story without seeing its satisfying end.

RE-ENVISION THE STORYLINE

When we fix our attention on all the ups and downs in the middle of the story, we easily despair. Our prayers, like David's at the beginning of this psalm, may be filled with anxiety, fear, and bitterness. In his mercy, God sometimes answers them. But he seems to respond much more readily to the tone of prayer David chose at the end—songs of gratitude. David shifted from hopelessness to praise.

Refuse to add hopelessness to your prayers. One of the hardest things to do when you're desperate is to worship God with gratitude, yet it's a vital shift that must take place in the heart for prayers to be powerful and full of faith. One of the best ways to make that shift is to envision the end of the story. Savor it. God has given us many promises; focus on them. When they fill your gaze, gratitude flows, faith rises, and God's goodness becomes much easier to see.

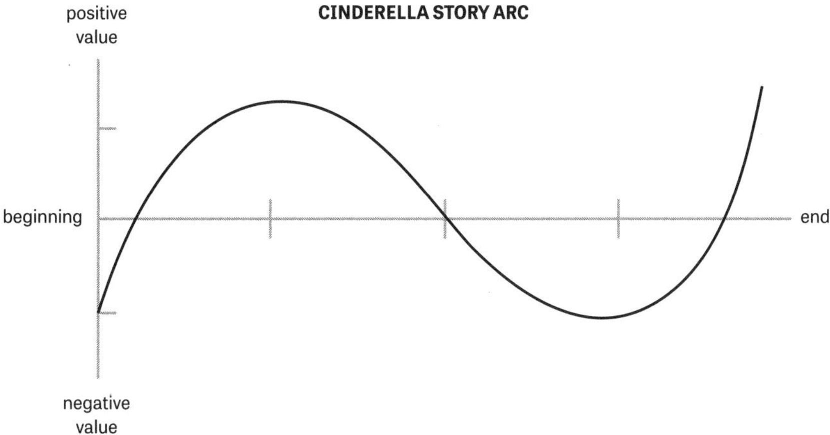

Fiction writers know that in the best stories, the protagonist is put through increasingly impossible situations until the breakthrough at the end. If we view many parts of the storyline other than the end, they look bleak and depressing. But knowing the end—and that God authors really good stories—changes everything we feel about the plot.

PSALM 14: FOR FOOLS TO SEE

God is with the generation of the righteous.

14:5, NKJV

The biblical psalms were written across several centuries, but always in the context of the formation of God's Kingdom through Israel at one stage or another. In every period, denying the existence or relevance of God—whether in favor of some other deity or not—was antithetical to the Kingdom itself. It was a rejection of God's plan for his people.

It was also very foolish (v. 1). We read this verse through the lenses of a culture well acquainted with atheism and agnosticism, philosophical positions foreign to most of the ancient world. But the psalmist wrote that the fool literally says, "There is no Elohim"—an apparent denial of Israel's faith, not necessarily of other gods. (This psalm uses the name *Yahweh* after v. 1; Psalm 53, a parallel psalm, uses the more general *Elohim* throughout.) Those who reject the one true God demonstrate fallen humanity's tendency toward idolatry. On this rebellious planet, the heart leans toward whichever gods will cater to it.

No wonder Paul quoted so liberally from this psalm (and others) to demonstrate the sinfulness and corruption of humanity (Romans 3:10-12). None are righteous; all have gone astray. Even those who have set their hearts on God's words and ways have inevitably fallen short of them.

RE-ENVISION DEVOTION

You don't have to look hard to see the enmity between those who commit to God's truth and those who don't. Psalm 1 placed them on opposite paths, and the differences show up in personal conflicts, culture wars, and everything in between. In those conflicts, never lose sight of God's assurances for those who deny their idols and cling to him. Though none are truly righteous, God has bound himself to those who seek his righteousness. He has also bound us to each other. Your faith is not just about you; it's about the Kingdom and its influence in this world. God responds to the faith of his people by filling them with his presence and power. And sometimes, eventually, even a fool can see that.

Who may worship in your sanctuary, LORD? Who may enter your presence on your holy hill?

15:1

An earlier psalm established that evil cannot dwell (literally, "sojourn") with God (5:4, ESV), and hearts filled with sin wouldn't want to anyway. But what about those who long for his presence—those like Moses and Joshua, who lingered with him in the Tabernacle? Or David, whose passion to establish a "house" for God in Jerusalem shaped Israel's (and the world's) history forever? What kind of person craves God's presence and is welcomed into it?

This psalm's answer is those with "blameless lives" (v. 2). Our hearts may sink at that—which of us is blameless? But the word translated here as "blameless" is used elsewhere to describe those headed in the right direction or those with integrity (for example, Proverbs 2:7, 21; 11:3, 20; 28:6, 10, 18). God welcomes people with strong ethics and hearts inclined toward him.

Of course, anyone can worship God in the sense of praising him. But here worship means something more: abiding with him, dwelling in his presence, soaking in the atmosphere he creates. The issue has nothing to do with rituals or songs but rather with being comfortable in his living room. Who does he want to hang out with? Certainly not those righteous enough to deserve his attention—no one qualifies for that—but those who long for his fellowship and are willing to fit in to the Kingdom environment.

RE-ENVISION WORSHIP

You'll need to be intentional about cultivating the environment of heaven within you and aligning your heart with God's. Worship is never an obligation, an exercise in loyalty, a mere ritual, or even just a good thing to do. It's a connection, a bonding moment, a matter of getting in sync with God, absorbing his nature and soaking in his presence. We begin to act like those we spend time with; if anyone is going to rub off on us, we want it to be him. Our worship draws us into his presence and draws his presence into our world. Those who ascend his "holy hill" find him descending into every area of their lives.

The land you have given me is a pleasant land. What a wonderful inheritance!

16:6

In the kingdom of Israel, land was a big deal. That was perhaps true everywhere, but in Israel it wasn't just land; it was *promised* land, part of a sacred covenant, an inheritance for all generations to come. Inheritance was about more than making a living or preserving the family's wealth. It was a matter of preserving each family's piece of the promise.

The "godly people in the land" (v. 3) did not "chase after other gods" (v. 4), as so many had done and would continue to do for centuries. God's plan was for his people to establish his worship in the place he had given them, inhabitants in a land devoted to him, in order to be a global testimony, his firstborn of many nations (Exodus 4:22). That's the commitment of this psalm, though enemies and idolaters were corrupting the inheritance and trampling on the promise. Still, God set the feet of his people in pleasant places. He promised a wonderful inheritance in spite of those who would abuse it. And he preserved a legacy of shalom—fullness, wholeness, peace—for those whose hearts were inclined toward his.

RE-ENVISION YOUR LEGACY

Inspired by seeing the age-old, everlasting Kingdom breaking into this world in a new way, Peter quoted this psalm at Pentecost (Acts 2:25-28). By design, that Kingdom is filled with God's presence, where there's "fullness of joy" and pleasures that never end (Psalm 16:11, NKJV). Israel's inheritance—and ours—was always going to be bigger than a plot of land or even a nation.

In all your struggles, don't forget to lift your eyes to see God's goodness. Bask in the blessings and favor he bestows on those who love him. Expand your vision to see beyond your personal relationship with him. You aren't just making an impact in your generation; you're building a legacy, an inheritance—a piece of the promise the ancient Israelites scarcely could have imagined—and that never fades away (Hebrews 11:13-16).

PSALM 17: THROUGH A LENS OF LOVE

Show me your unfailing love in wonderful ways.

17:7

Many psalms position the psalmist at the point of a triangle facing the two other points: adversaries and God. Because this standoff takes place in the context of a divinely established covenant, the psalmist appeals to God on those terms. The enemies aren't keeping the covenant; the psalmist is. Therefore, he can count on God to be faithful. When under attack, he assumes God will take his side.

So much of this psalm is based on the innocence and righteousness of the psalmist that we can hardly relate to it. But context matters. It may have been written on one of the many occasions David was being falsely accused—perhaps while running from Saul, his life under constant threat, or perhaps while under attack from Absalom's faction. If so, David is simply asserting that in the matter of slander against him, he is innocent. He is trusting that God defends the one whose cause is right.

He is also expressing faith that he will wake up alive (v. 15)—a notion that, at least in his earthly life, was not a given, considering the violence threatened against him at times. In spite of his imperfections, he knows God plans a hope-filled future for him.

RE-ENVISION ADVERSITY

In difficult times, humans often instinctively cast God as one who angrily withholds blessings until we do better. David didn't buy into that formula. His conscience was clear, yet his trials were still intense. He didn't view circumstances as a direct statement of God's favor. He saw God's goodness and knew God wanted to demonstrate his love in wonderful ways.

Live with that assumption of God's goodness. Refuse to see his love through the lens of your adversity; instead, see your adversity through the lens of his love. See yourself as "the apple of [his] eye" (v. 8, NKJV; literally "pupil"). However unworthy you feel, let God delight in you. In any triangle involving opposition, he always takes the side of his faithful ones.

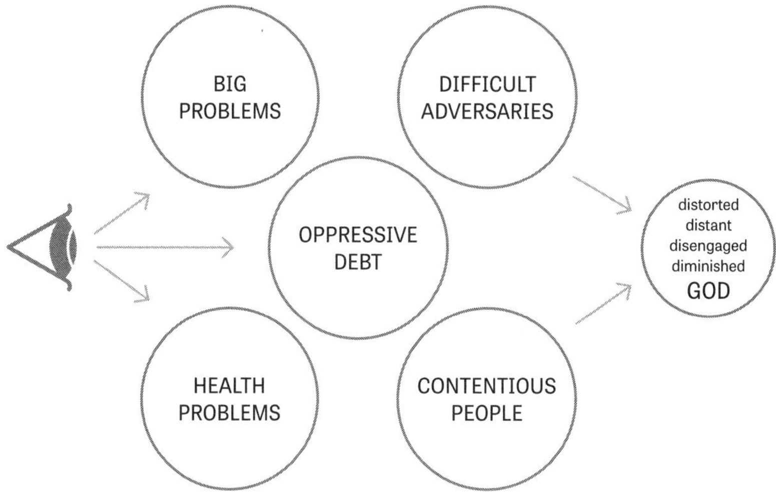

Looking through the right lens: When we see God through the lenses of our circumstances, he appears distant and detached, and our circumstances appear huge. When we see our circumstances through the lens of God, he is magnified in our hearts and minds, and our circumstances resume their true appearance. Our faith weakens or strengthens according to the lenses we look through.

PSALM 18: THE ULTIMATE ANSWER TO PRAYER

God's way is perfect. All the LORD's promises prove true. He is a shield for all who look to him for protection.

18:30

The king had been delivered from all his enemies, including from Saul (see a variation of this psalm in 2 Samuel 22). But Psalm 18:50 mentions God's "anointed," which can refer to both the king as God's anointed and—ultimately—the Messiah (which means, literally, "anointed one"). In each case, the anointed was delivered from the ropes of death that entangled him, the deliverance was thunderous and earthshaking, and God delighted in the innocence of the anointed one he saved from destruction and death. In dramatic, history-shaping ways, God came through.

This isn't just the story of a king and the Messiah. It's also an invitation for all God's people to experience the same dramatic deliverance. Those who are in Christ have the Spirit of the Anointed One in them and, by implication, are anointed ones too (2 Corinthians 1:21-22; 1 John 2:27). Like David and Jesus, we can expect God to defend us. As members of his royal priesthood, we can call on him and expect him to answer—sometimes as powerfully and dramatically as in this psalm.

Of course, David's deliverance played out over years. Ours may too. But God is with us through it all. His arm is never too short, his delight in his children never fades, and his promises never expire. He is willing to shake the earth to defend and preserve his people.

RE-ENVISION YOUR PRAYERS

You may not notice the earth shaking when you pray; natural eyes can't perceive God working behind the scenes or trust his answers when visual evidence seems to contradict his work. But eyes of faith can, and if you cultivate your spiritual vision, you can pray with assurance that the unseen stage is filled with dramatic movements. Like Elisha's servant (2 Kings 6:17), let your eyes be opened to the angelic armies and thunderous responses of God. Heaven moves when the prayers of God's people converge with his power and purposes.

TORAH PSALMS

Covenants are in the background of many psalms, although it's not always clear which covenant is in view. God made several covenants with his people throughout their history, each building on previous ones. In his covenant with Abraham, God promised to multiply Abraham's descendants and bless all the families of the earth through him (Genesis 12:1-3). His covenant given through Moses included the law (often referred to as the Torah), along with numerous blessings for obedience and curses for disobedience (Leviticus 26; Deuteronomy 28). And in his covenant with David, God promised to establish David's throne as an everlasting dynasty (2 Samuel 7:1-17). All these covenants are thoroughly embedded in the understanding of the psalmists.

These covenants serve as the backdrop for numerous psalms, but three psalms specifically exalt the Torah (Psalms 1, 19, and 119). They focus on the law and all its benefits, referring to it by various terms, which can be translated "commandments," "statutes," "testimonies," and "precepts," among other similar words. In each case, these psalms are paired with a messianic psalm (Psalms 2, 18, and 118), highlighting both God's perfect standards and his mercy and grace when we fall short of them. (There's a subtle but frequent juxtaposition of law and grace in Scripture.)

In these Torah psalms, as well as others that focus on wisdom and truth, God's law (or better, "instruction") is praised for its perfection, power, and purpose. It nourishes human souls and keeps us from evil. It also reveals the leanings of our hearts. Those who love God cling to his words; those who don't ignore them.

We might describe God's Word differently today—not primarily in terms of Torah observance but primarily in terms of how it reveals who he is and who we are in relation to him. But the thought is the same: His revelation gives us life. As the first psalm assures us, those who delight in it are blessed.

PSALM 19: CHOOSE YOUR VISION

May the words of my mouth and the meditation of my heart be pleasing to you, O LORD, my rock and my redeemer.

19:14

Just as Psalms 1 and 2 paired a messianic psalm with a Torah psalm, so do Psalms 18 and 19. Here the treatment of Torah shifts for the rest of Book 1. Teaching, guidance, and confession are increasingly emphasized as God, the Rock of his people (18:2, 46), instructs them in the ways they should go.*

But it isn't only the written law that proclaims God's truth. So do the heavens (19:1). Like a radiant bridegroom, the sun bursts forth, shining light on all God has made (v. 5). Those with eyes of faith can see what is plainly revealed, and the Lord cleanses us from the hidden sins lurking in our hearts (v. 12). Like Paul (Romans 1:20), the psalmist is well aware that creation and the Word are testimonies of God's presence, wisdom, power, and love. And he wants to align himself with the Source.

Astonishingly, the eyes of faith and the eyes of faithlessness can observe the same scenes and read the same words while seeing completely different things. In one vision, God is obvious. In the other, he's invisible or irrelevant. The difference is not in the object but in the choices of the observer. Not everyone wants eyes to see and ears to hear (Matthew 13:15-16).

* Robertson, *Flow of the Psalms*, 73–78.

RE-ENVISION YOUR PREOCCUPATIONS

We were designed to be overwhelmed by something, but we get to choose what will overwhelm us. Will it be our workload or bills, hopes and dreams for what hasn't happened yet, complicated relationships, or some other crisis that weighs us down? Or will it be God's glory that constantly pours forth from the heavens? One preoccupation leads to discouragement, bitterness, and death; the other leads to peace, joy, and life—and to thoughts and words that align with God's. His glory is life-changing, but only if we can see it. And seeing it is a lifestyle we can choose any moment of any day.

PSALM 20: A ROYAL IDENTITY

May he grant your heart's desires and make all your plans succeed. . . . May the Lord answer all your prayers.

20:4-5

Before Jehoshaphat went out to battle, he sent singers to walk ahead of the army and proclaim God's enduring love (2 Chronicles 20:21). The situation was dire—Jerusalem was surrounded by a coalition of three armies, a sitting duck in the turbulent waters of that era's geopolitical pond—and prophetic inspiration had urged worship ahead of battle. As so often happens in God's Kingdom, praise comes before victories.

This psalm and the next may have been used in similar ways.* These psalms "of David" are apparently more *about* him; one offering prayer that the king's plans would succeed, the other celebrating that they did. These royal psalms, which appeal confidently to God in his sanctuary to hear and help, also bless the messianic king.

Royal psalms in the Hebrew context are all about the king—though the welfare of the people is directly tied to the welfare of the king, and in that sense, they are about the kingdom as a whole. But New Testament theology places every believer "in Christ" as a participant in his reign and a co-heir of his victories (see Romans 8:17). For "a royal priesthood" (1 Peter 2:9, NIV), *royal*

* Gerald H. Wilson, *Psalms*, vol. 1, NIVAC (Grand Rapids: Zondervan, 2002), 381–382.

takes on a rather democratic reach. As sons and daughters of the King, we can receive the blessings in Scripture that are given to him.

RE-ENVISION YOUR IDENTITY

Do you see yourself more as a subject of the King or a member of the royal family? In truth, you're both, but many believers see only their servanthood, not their royalty. When we fail to recognize how thoroughly we've been adopted into the King's family, we begin to think we're on our own. We risk trusting in horses and chariots rather than the family name (Psalm 20:7). Without any real authority behind us, we think it's up to us to make things happen.

Ask for a bigger, nobler vision. Recognize who you are in Christ. Pray with royal authority. And confidently trust that God is willing to fulfill the desires he has placed within your heart.

PSALM 21: ROYAL VICTORIES

You have given him his heart's desire; you have withheld nothing he requested.

21:2

Imagine having this psalm prayed on your behalf. It is full of gratitude for what God has done and how he has crowned his servant-king, granted him life and glory, subdued all his enemies, and given him his heart's desire. Where the previous psalm anticipated God's fulfillment, this one celebrates it. God's purposes have been thoroughly, extravagantly accomplished, to the delight of the king.

Why did God give the king such success and prosperity, a crown of finest gold, long life, splendor and majesty, eternal blessings, and the joy of God's presence (vv. 3-6)? Because the king trusted God (v. 7). That's the catalyst. God responds to those whose hearts are fully his (see 2 Chronicles 16:9).

This wasn't just a passive trust. It was forged in the trenches as David was pursued throughout the kingdom, his life constantly on the line. It was put-your-money-where-your-mouth-is trust, the kind made visible when most are tempted to lose heart. Regardless of which victory this psalm is celebrating, it came at a cost. All victories do. But when God is their author, they are thorough and complete.

RE-ENVISION GOD'S INTENTIONS

As we've seen, royal psalms can apply to members of the royal family—which now includes all who are in Christ by faith. Their words may seem too extravagant for us common folk, but we are not so common. God has shared with us his great and precious promises and his own divine nature (2 Peter 1:3-4). If we are committed to the royal agenda—if we live with a Kingdom mindset—he will grant us royal victories.

Do you see him as the God who gives you only what you need and rarely something more? If so, recast your vision. He *wants* to bless you with good things—spiritually to be sure, but in tangible ways too. He is not a hard master, not obsessed with disciplining you (though he will at times), not a vegetables-only-and-never-dessert kind of Father. He generally wants to give more than our faith will receive, on several fronts, especially for the advance of his Kingdom. Let him.

PSALM 22: GOD ENTHRONED

You are holy, enthroned on the praises of Israel.

22:3

When Jesus quoted this psalm from the cross (Matthew 27:46), he was invoking the whole psalm, not just the first line. For a moment, he was abandoned, forsaken, made to carry sin for a world incapable of carrying it on its own. Though these words are attributed to David's pen, they came from the inspiration of the Spirit and pointed toward the Messiah's greatest sacrifice and victory. David's pain and promise were taken up by the Savior and became the world's.

This psalm is a lament that God's presence seems completely absent during a season of suffering. It prophesies of Jesus' suffering quite specifically, but it was written by someone going through similar agony—and God was not intervening as expected. In fact, God was nowhere to be found in the midst of the pain. But from that despair came a remarkable remembrance, a truth about where God is even when we can't sense him: He is enthroned on the praises of his people.

Because of that, the psalm ends with assurance: God's righteous acts would be told for generations to come (v. 31). Even when he seems distant and disinterested, he is still at work.

RE-ENVISION YOUR PRAISE

God is on his throne all the time. Our praises do not put him there. But they do "enthrone" him in situations where he seems absent or displaced by an unholy presence. When chaos seems to reign, praise reestablishes God's reign over it. As carriers of his person and presence, we have a lot to say about how his rule manifests in our world.

Catch a vision for how your worship connects with God's manifest presence, even when you don't sense him or can't see his power at work. Let your heart and words enthrone him in every area of your life and the world around you. Even when he seems far away, he is powerfully and purposefully present in your worship. Chaos, confusion, and conflict must bow before his throne.

PSALM 23: UNDER HIS WATCH

Surely your goodness and unfailing love will pursue me all the days of my life.

23:6

When the elders of Israel gathered at Hebron to affirm David as king, they saw David as a shepherd who would rule the people as his flock (2 Samuel 5:2). The image went back to the patriarchs—Jacob once spoke of God as his shepherd (Genesis 48:15-16). And it looked far into the future—prophets condemned the kingdom's abusive shepherds and promised competent, compassionate ones (Jeremiah 3:14-15; 10:21; 23:1-8; Ezekiel 34:1-24). Here, David uses that imagery for God, the Good Shepherd. Jesus would later apply the same image to himself (John 10:11-18).

The beauty of this image of the Shepherd-King is that it captures the tenderness, protection, correction, provision, and attentiveness of God for his often dense, directionless people. He not only cares for us; he brings us to fertile fields and fresh waters and guides us through dark valleys. As a royal host, he even prepares a feast for us right in front of our enemies. Those who want us to fail have to watch us succeed. Those who curse us have to see us blessed. God's goodness and love don't just wait for us. They pursue us as long as we live.

RE-ENVISION THE PURSUIT

If any psalm points us to a new vision, it's this one. That's its whole point. Instead of seeing a king who demands servitude, we see a King who tenderly watches over his sheep. Instead of living in an every-man-for-himself world, we see pastures and streams simply given to us. Instead of constantly pursuing the peace and abundance we crave, we see goodness and love pursuing us relentlessly. Even for many people who have quoted this psalm often, it's still an image that hasn't entirely sunk in. It's one thing to know this about God, another to live as though it's true. The sheep in his fold and the guests at his table have nothing to worry about and everything to gain. We can simply enjoy the rest, the feasting, and the presence of the Shepherd-King.

Who is the King of glory? The LORD, strong and mighty; the LORD, invincible in battle.

24:8

This processional hymn opens with a declaration that the entire world—from the oceans' depths to the people on every land—is God's domain. From there, all the action converges on the place of worship, the spiritual center of life. In David's day, that would be the Tabernacle; in later history, the Temple; and still later, wherever the Spirit of God resides, including human hearts. This celebrated King of glory is not just Israel's but the world's.

Like Psalm 15, this psalm asks who may ascend to God's holy place to worship him. The answer again includes those with pure hearts and truthful lips. It isn't that others aren't qualified to seek him—anyone can, as the rest of Scripture makes abundantly clear—but dwelling with him goes beyond mere seeking. We enter deep fellowship with God by synchronizing our heartbeat with his. By his grace and through his Spirit, we become more like him.

The psalm ends with an invitation to the King of glory to come in. It may portray priests leading the Ark of the Covenant to the Tabernacle (perhaps returning it after a successful battle) and the priest at the gates welcoming God's presence in.* But more figuratively it represents the joyful meeting

* Tremper Longman III, *Psalms: An Introduction and Commentary*, TOTC 15–16 (Downers Grove, IL: IVP Academic, 2014), 141.

of God and the worshiper in the place of his presence. That's where battles are won, enemies are overcome, and victories are celebrated. It's the fellowship of fulfillment.

RE-ENVISION YOUR AUDIENCE

When you worship, how do you envision God responding? Is he listening with interest or with a raised eyebrow? Does he casually receive your worship, perhaps unmoved by it? Or does he enter his throne room with joy, fanfare, and the promises and power to accomplish resounding victories on your behalf? Worship intensifies the more clearly you know the audience receiving it, and according to this psalm, your audience is the strong and mighty King of glory heartily responding to your praise. He is no passive receiver of your worship; he warmly welcomes you into his presence. Welcome him into yours, and open your entire being to the glory he brings.

PSALM 25: THE BURDEN-BEARER

No one who trusts in you will ever be disgraced.

25:3

Some psalms begin with a crisis. There's one here, too—the psalmist is "alone and in deep distress" (v. 16)—but that's not the anchor point for this plea. Before any complaints or laments comes a statement of implicit trust (vv. 1-2), a statement that's repeated often in various forms. Although undergoing a severe trial, the psalmist is supremely confident. What appears awful is surely only temporary and still clearly subject to God's goodness and love.

In spite of his many sins (vv. 7, 11), the psalmist knows that no one who trusts God will be disgraced. Though being accused or threatened by vicious people—that happened a lot with David—the psalmist is secure in his position and apparently affirms his hope throughout the crisis. The prayer's acrostic structure makes it memorable. Reminding ourselves of God's faithfulness, his promises, and his character is always a powerful antidote to fear, anxiety, and doubt.

RE-ENVISION YOUR BURDEN

The enemy of your soul loves to discourage you. He will point to some past experience and say, "Look at how badly you failed!" But God will say of the same experience, "Look at what you overcame!" The psalmist could have assumed he was being punished for his sin, or that his enemies had the upper hand, or that his shame and disgrace defined him; but he assumed instead that he would be rescued and vindicated. Natural eyes might have a false vision of God in this kind of situation, but eyes of faith see his goodness above all.

Because God is good and does what is right (v. 9), the resolution to this crisis comes from him, not us. That's where we need to focus our vision. We understand that he carries the weight of salvation—that's what the gospel of grace is all about—but we often forget that he also carries the weight of our daily burdens (1 Peter 5:7). We know he is good; we need to see him as good *to us*. All our guilt, failures, and trials look different in light of his faithfulness.

I wash my hands to declare my innocence. I come to your altar, O LORD, singing a song of thanksgiving and telling of all your wonders.

26:6-7

Book 1 of the Psalms is filled with references to God's "house" or "sanctuary." Historically this refers to the Temple in Jerusalem, but in the psalms authored by David, it refers to the Tabernacle since the Temple was not yet built. In any case, this sanctuary is the center of spiritual life, for both the individual and the community. And it's where the tension-filled triangle between the petitioner, his enemies, and God plays out repeatedly. In the many crises and conflicts of these psalms, the psalmist knows only one place to go for resolution: God's presence.

That's why he comes to the altar singing songs of thanksgiving and telling of God's wonders, and why he declares his love for the sanctuary where God's "glorious presence dwells" (v. 8). He knows where God lands on this issue between the godly and the treacherous. The Torah and the first psalm have made that clear. There is a distinct choice between two groups of people, and God is taking sides. If we're shaped by the people we spend time with, we need to take sides too. David does so rather emphatically in verse 11, committing to a life of integrity and distancing himself from sinful schemers. He chooses to dwell with God in the place of glory.

RE-ENVISION YOUR GOALS

What do you envision getting out of life? What do you spend your days striving for? If dwelling in God's glory and presence isn't at the forefront of your vision—and if we're honest, most of us often let it slip to the back of our minds—you're missing your created purpose. Filling our eyes with something other than the pursuit of his presence is the root of futility and frustration. But when experiencing his presence is our highest goal, enemies and obstacles fade into the background. It's the vision we were created for. It fills us with life and adventure, and it's where all his "wonders" begin.

PSALM 27: THE LONG VIEW

I am confident I will see the LORD's goodness while I am here in the land of the living.

27:13

In a psalm full of memorable, life-anchoring verses, one theme stands out: seeing the big picture rather than immediate circumstances. Though enemies and armies are ready to devour the righteous (vv. 2-3, 11-12), why fear? Though rejection and betrayal are part of life (vv. 9-10), why be insecure? Though people whose hearts hunger to bask in God's presence (vv. 4-5) have not seen the completion of the Temple—which was true in David's case—why lament? God promises deliverance, draws near to the oppressed and rejected, and establishes his presence with his people wherever they are. Whatever the situations before us say, that is never the final word. He is.

That's why David was confident he would see God's goodness in the land of the living—this side of eternity. Yes, he had experienced threats, betrayal, and slander, but he had also received God's promises, including one for a Temple to be built by his son. David's deep longing, seen in verse 4, would remain unsatisfied to a point; he would never set foot in the Temple, though he could worship in the Tabernacle and still, as an act of faith, prepare for the Temple until the day he died. In spite of all his adversity, he knew life was more than a series of setbacks. He could "wait patiently for the LORD" (v. 14) and know the wait would be worth it.

RE-ENVISION HIS BLESSINGS

Some people see life as arduous and heaven as their only relief. But God provides seasons of refreshment and restoration here and now, not just there and then. The problem is that we often give up on this vision of faith after a few days or weeks of suffering; or sometimes we judge God by how quickly or clearly he responds. Scripture emphatically gives us the long view. We can't afford to make judgments in the middle of the story; we have to trust that the end of it will be good. That takes patience and courage, but those who cling to both will see God's goodness in the land of the living.

PAIN AND ADVERSITY NOW | GOD'S GOODNESS IN ETERNITY

Many committed believers unconsciously assume that this life will be filled with hardship and all (or almost all) of God's blessings are reserved for heaven.

PAIN AND ADVERSITY NOW

GOD'S GOODNESS NOW AND IN ETERNITY

In reality, God's blessings begin now, "in the land of the living." Even though we still experience hardship until we get to heaven, God promises we will experience many of eternity's joys in this age.

PSALM 28: A STAGE FOR REVELATION

He helps me, and my heart is filled with joy. I burst out in songs of thanksgiving.

28:7

Like so many psalms, this one begins in crisis and need, features a cry for help backed by statements of faith, and results in deliverance. Here the rescue is certain and seems to have already happened. In other psalms, deliverance has not come by the end, yet the psalmist knows that it will. Whether or not the psalmist has gotten there on the timeline, his heart can be filled with joy and his mouth with songs of gratitude.

We might wonder, though: If God can so powerfully rescue his people, why doesn't he just keep them out of trouble in the first place? Why must the drama of deliverance play out? We may never know all the reasons, but we can see a clear connection between our predicaments and his desire to intervene—how our need sets the stage for him to demonstrate who he is. Our crises create a platform for him to reveal his nature. Who would ever see his mercy if no one needed it? What does unconditional love look like when no conditions are there? How can God be known as Healer if no one is sick, or Deliverer if no one was ever captive? If his full nature is to be revealed, there have to be circumstances that highlight it.

RE-ENVISION YOUR SUFFERING

Your suffering is not just about you. Learn to see it in a larger context—an ongoing cosmic revelation of God's divine attributes that, apart from a fallen world, might remain forever hidden. That vision changes our questions. Instead of simply "why me?" or "how long?" we begin to ask, "Lord, what do you want to do here? How do you want to display yourself? Which characteristic do you want to show?" Our problems become an occasion for God's solutions. We experience his nature. Suffering that was once a burden becomes a remarkable opportunity for us to see him at work—and for a watching world to see him too.

PSALM 29: GOD OF GLORY

The voice of the LORD strikes with bolts of lightning . . . makes the barren wilderness quake . . . twists mighty oaks and strips the forests bare. In his Temple everyone shouts, "Glory!"

29:7-9

This psalm depicts a violent storm, using language common to Canaanite poetry. But there may be a pointed purpose in such language. Some of Israel's idolaters might have attributed those ferocious elements of nature to the Canaanite storm god Baal, but in reality, a much greater God commands and controls them merely with his voice. He doesn't strain to churn up lightning, thunder, violent waves, earthquakes, and powerful winds. He doesn't struggle to handle mountains and oceans. He just speaks, and his awesome power is released.

This psalm is set in the heavenly realms. Angelic beings and supposed deities are told to observe the majesty of this God and be awed. Though his power is above the elements, not competing with them, it also fills the earthly realm, where storms actually occur. In the midst of it all, everyone in God's temple shouts, "Glory!" We are left to wonder: Which temple? The one in Jerusalem where Israelites worshiped, or perhaps one in heaven where angels and other heavenly observers witness God's glory (as in Revelation 11:19)? Scripture affirms both, and the psalm hints at each. We may conclude that God is being recognized where those realms intersect. Unlike any storm god, the God of Israel fills both heaven and earth.

RE-ENVISION YOUR RESIDENCE

Few people today are tempted to make sacrifices to a Canaanite storm god to curry favor or avoid divine consequences. But many embrace a materialistic worldview that sees everything as simply natural. As believers, we're called to walk in two realms at once: the natural and the supernatural, where the God of glory does miraculous works but also holds thunderous natural forces in his hand. The human heart longs for a connection between heaven and earth, and as a citizen of one and a resident of the other, you're it—a bridge between the God of glory and humans living in resignation to what befalls them in a natural, materialistic world. Pray his glory down, lift people up to him, and bless heaven and earth with his power and peace.

PSALM 30: LIVING IN THE YES

You have turned my mourning into joyful dancing.

30:11

The superscription of this psalm says it was written by David for the dedication of the Temple. If not a later addition (as many scholars believe), this line tells us a lot about him. Rescue from death, as described in this psalm—whether a deliverance from violent enemies or physical illness—is a major theme in his life, which was filled with dangers but also divine protection. David was chosen, anointed, protected, enthroned, established, forgiven, and promised an everlasting dynasty. And every step of the way was divinely ordained, allowed, and compensated for. He had to have seen it all as miraculous.

The theme of rescue shapes this dedication for the Temple, David's deepest longing. David could have grown bitterly disappointed when God said the Temple would be built by his son, but instead he did everything he could to prepare for it without actually laying stone upon stone. In addition to setting up the entire worship apparatus and culture with priests, musicians, and other Temple personnel, he raised money, gathered materials, drew up plans, rallied a workforce, and wrote this dedicatory psalm (1 Chronicles 22–29). What could have been an occasion for mourning—not being able to fulfill his dream—became an occasion for dancing. After all, the Temple would be built, even if his eyes would never see it.

RE-ENVISION GOD'S YES

David had experienced God's anger and was well-acquainted with tears, yet he knew that God's favor lasts a lifetime and that his joy comes with the morning (Psalm 30:5). As Christians, many of us focus on God's no, and then we tend to get stuck in our disappointments. But mature faith rides the wave of whatever yes he has given us. Hearts captivated by a big enough yes have little trouble handling a no. We embrace what is given and let go of what isn't. We fill ourselves with hope and expectation, produce fruit wherever yes takes us, and live with gratitude and joy. Our mourning turns to dancing, our silence turns to praise, and we realize just how much God has blessed us.

PSALM 31: A STOREHOUSE OF GOODNESS

How great is the goodness you have stored up for those who fear you. You lavish it on those who come to you for protection, blessing them before the watching world.

31:19

On the surface, the cry of this psalm comes from within the walls of a city under siege (v. 21). In such circumstances, the pressures would be enormous—an existential threat coming from beyond the walls, with rampant discontent and complaining within them. For most people, these are not the conditions that stir up faith and gratitude. Yet both are clearly expressed in this psalm.

In spite of the enormity of the threat, the psalmist is convinced that God hides his people in the shelter of his presence, "safe from those who conspire against them . . . far from accusing tongues" (v. 20). The psalmist has heard the rumors and conspiracies (v. 13), yet he declares that God is his strength and commits his spirit into God's hands (v. 5), a line quoted by Jesus at his moment of death (Luke 23:46). Amid all the dreadful things that could happen not only to the psalmist but also to the men, women, and children of his city if it is captured, he turns his attention to the goodness of God stored up for those who fear him. He trusts that God will intervene.

RE-ENVISION THE SITUATION

That wasn't his first reaction. He initially panicked (Psalm 31:2; see also vv. 9-10). His natural eyes saw warriors, idolaters, and accusers—a complete contrast to what God had promised in his covenant with him and his people—and the outcome appeared catastrophic. But behind the scenes, he saw a God who delivers his people out of trouble, keeps his promises, and hides his loved ones in his shelter. Panic was replaced by conviction (vv. 14-15). In light of God's promises, being strong and courageous made more sense.

When you're presented with competing visions—the threat before your eyes versus the assurances of God—you can know which one is dominant by whether you're afraid or at peace. If you aren't at peace, refocus. Look behind the scenes to the goodness God has stored up for those who trust him, and rest in it by faith.

PENITENTIAL PSALMS

Though the theme of repentance appears in many psalms, seven in particular have historically been known as "penitential psalms." The Roman Catholic Church has identified these as Psalms 6, 32, 38, 51, 102, 130, and 143. Protestants often prefer the term "psalms of repentance" and sometimes expand the list to include 7, 25, 39–41, 65, 78, 85, and 106—essentially any psalm that includes some form of confession and a plea for forgiveness. But with many psalms, categories are imprecise.

Penance and repentance are not the same thing. The former emphasizes the sinner's efforts to be forgiven or make up for sin; the latter, while including a turning from sin, emphasizes God's forgiveness. A repentant heart recognizes that we can't atone for our own sin; only God can forgive it. So the term *penitential* is somewhat inaccurate; most of these psalms include nothing resembling penance or an effort to make up for past sins (though some do include vows). These psalms do express genuine grief over failures and offenses and a longing for restoration and reconciliation with God.

Of course, the goal in reading Psalms is not to figure out their genre or type but to find expression for our very human experiences and receive revelation from God on how to connect with him in every circumstance of our lives. For that, the many expressions of repentance throughout the Psalms provide encouraging models of humility and comforting assurances of God's mercy, redemption, and restoration.

What joy for those whose record the Lord has cleared of guilt, whose lives are lived in complete honesty!

32:2

This psalm is a profound expression of repentance. We don't know which sin was at issue here, unlike Psalm 51, which clearly identifies the occasion as David's repentance for his adultery with Bathsheba. But whatever it was, keeping quiet about it was emotionally and physically agonizing, and confessing it was liberating. The psalmist felt a crushing burden at the beginning of the psalm, then no longer felt the weight of guilt by the end of it.

What happened between that crushing burden and the freedom of casting it off? The only catalyst for that transition from agony to joy was being honest about the sin (v. 5). The psalmist confessed it to God (and perhaps others), and with no exercises of penance or efforts to spiritually compensate for it, the guilt was gone. God simply forgave him. And for that, he could declare a blessing on those whose lives are lived in complete honesty.

RE-ENVISION YOURSELF

Some of us feel a need to keep confessing and repenting for everything in our past—so much brokenness, guilt, and shame; so many misunderstandings, offenses, and embarrassments; and so much pain. It's good to go through moments or seasons of deep repentance, but after honest confession, there comes a time to move on—permanently. God does not want his children to dwell in their brokenness. He never calls us to live sin-focused lives.

The whole point of redemption and restoration is to get us out of that condition, not to remain stuck in our sins and the pain that comes from them. God thoroughly cleanses us and wants us to see ourselves as new creations (see 2 Corinthians 5:17). If, in his mind, he removes our sins from us as far as the east is from the west (Psalm 103:12), it makes little sense to keep them close in our minds. Our broken past is meant to fade into a distant memory, if a memory at all, so we can live with clean consciences and new, wonder-filled eyes.

The LORD's plans stand firm forever; his intentions can never be shaken.

33:11

This psalm of celebration is filled with praise. Absent are the enemies, threats, accusations, slanders, diseases, and sins that have filled many psalms up to this point. Here is a call to worship with voices and instruments, to recognize the awesome power of the God who created the vast universe with the sound of his voice, to admire his governance of the nations, and to appreciate his thorough knowledge of human nature. He is good in everything he does, and his love for his people never fails.

Why the exuberance? No occasion is given, though there are hints of a victory in battle. The appeal to "sing a new song" (v. 3) is scattered throughout Scripture, always in the context of warfare, as if God's victory prompts a new beginning.* But more generally, this psalm incorporates themes of creation (vv. 6-9) and God's Kingdom (vv. 10-12), and, like so many others, a statement of trust and hope in the Lord. He doesn't just grant his people favor; he does the heavy lifting. At individual, national, and even global levels, the reasons to praise God are clear.

RE-ENVISION YOUR CALLING

Train yourself to see worship as your first and highest calling. You may have envisioned other callings or even prioritized them—if not in your theology,

* Longman, *Psalms*, 166.

at least in practice. But if you see yourself as something other than a worshiper first, your life will remain out of sync with your created purpose and with the rhythm of the universe. That may not be readily visible—the rest of the world is out of sync too—but it's true. All creation was designed to worship, glorify, and enjoy God. Let this psalm serve as a model. One of your greatest weapons against the kingdom of darkness is joy (see Nehemiah 8:10). Rejoice with all your heart and enjoy the victories that come.

Taste and see that the LORD is good. Oh, the joys of those who take refuge in him!

34:8

Early in his exile from Saul, David sought refuge in the Philistine city of Gath. The king's officials were suspicious of David's intentions, so he feigned insanity to demonstrate he was no threat, then moved on to find refuge in the cave of Adullam (1 Samuel 21:10–22:1). This psalm celebrates God's protection and deliverance during those disorienting, threatening times.

Not only are we told God is good; we're encouraged to experience his goodness ourselves. David invites us to "taste and see" and follows up the invitation with assurances that those who look to God will have all they need and will lack no good thing (Psalm 34:9-10). He promises that God is near to all his people, especially the brokenhearted (vv. 15-18). And he sweepingly affirms that even though the righteous face many troubles, God delivers them each time (v. 19).

RE-ENVISION HIS GOODNESS

This psalm literally invites us to re-envision God and test his promises out. Intellectually, we already grasp everything it says, but in our deep-down perceptions of God, the question of his goodness remains. This issue has caused a raging battle within us from day one—personally and as members of the human race (see Genesis 3:1-4). No matter how often we're told he's good, our souls whisper questions, especially in times of crisis and pain. *Will he really be that good to us?*

When you pray, do you see yourself sitting at the negotiating table across from God, pleading with him to intervene in your life? Or are you sitting on the same side next to God, facing the circumstances of your life together? Do you feel as if you have to twist his arm for your dreams and desires to be fulfilled, or are they seeds he has planted in your heart with the full intention of growing them to maturity and fruitfulness? The battle concerning his goodness plays out here, and only experience with him will convince us. In every situation, we are urged to "taste and see."

With every bone in my body I will praise him: "LORD, who can compare with you? Who else rescues the helpless from the strong?"

35:10

The survival of the fittest is the way of the world. The strong win, and the helpless suffer. This is how life works on a fallen, broken, rebellious planet—sometimes even in courts that supposedly administer justice.

That's the setting for this psalm—the psalmist is on trial, fighting false accusations and a presumption of guilt. The accusers are fierce, but even in the intensity of a legal battle, David vows to praise God for defending him. He may not be in a position to contend with those who accuse him, but God is. And even though he seems to be in a helpless situation, no one is helpless when God is their defender.

This psalm is largely a lament, but it's lined with faith and expectation. There is extreme frustration about how events have gone but also confidence in how they will turn out (along with a plea for them to turn out well). The curses against the psalmist's enemies may seem harsh (vv. 4-6, 8, 26), but they are in line with the blessings and curses God laid out in Leviticus 26 and Deuteronomy 28. The psalmist knows God's character and can trust him with his future. And he can marvel that God rescues the helpless from the strong.

RE-ENVISION YOUR ADVOCATE

When our reputation takes a hit, especially unfairly, we tend to feel like victims. Our natural eyes see only the persecution we are suffering. People with no regard for truth or integrity seem to have the upper hand, leaving us feeling defenseless, helpless, and mistreated. Our souls are plagued by fear, resentment, and bitterness.

The eyes of faith see something else: a God who defends his people and always comes down on the side of truth. Like David, we can go ahead and praise him in advance for the vindication that will surely come. In doing so, our souls return to confidence, peace, and trust because we know the truth: Sooner or later, our Defender will win his case.

You feed them from the abundance of your own house, letting them drink from your river of delights.

36:8

The world is full of people who have no heart for God. Multitudes have shut their ears to his voice and followed their own selfish agendas without regard for God's desires or anyone else's. Certainly not all unbelievers can be described so cynically, but many can. And the psalmist seems acutely aware of them.

The first and last sections of this psalm describe the world's aggression and deception, but the middle section offers a sharp contrast, as if God steps in to provide an oasis of truth and peace for his people. Creation is described in its original beauty, and from the Temple, a microcosm of creation, comes a river of delight for God's people to enjoy (vv. 5-9). Though the depth of human depravity is great, the depth of God's unfailing love—expressed in abundance, delights, and the light of life—is far greater, more than enough to overcome the destructive force of evil. No matter what plots conniving people come up with, God can unravel them. Nothing this world can throw at us outweighs what God promises to give us.

RE-ENVISION YOUR CHOICES

This psalm, like so many others, offers a clear choice of visions to focus on. We could fill our gaze with all that's going wrong and what people are doing to us, or we can fix our gaze on God's goodness. One choice leads to constant frustration, angst, hopelessness, and bitterness. The other leads to hopefulness and gratitude—even when the circumstances in both views are exactly the same. Perspective is a powerful thing.

You get to choose your vision. Will you dwell on those who cause harm and create chaos, or will you dwell on the Lord above them all? Will you drink from steady streams of a corrupt culture or gulp from the river of delight that flows from God's throne? It's not escapism—living in denial or fleeing worldly concerns—to choose the latter; it's embracing a deeper reality. Immerse yourself in the fountain of life and rest in God's vast, unfailing abundance and love.

Trust in the LORD and do good. Then you will live safely in the land and prosper. Take delight in the LORD, and he will give you your heart's desires.

37:3-4

God delivered his people, gave them a law full of spiritual and ethical standards, led them into the Land of Promise, and told them to be faithful in it. As we know, in spite of this unique calling as God's treasured possession, quite a few of them did not remain faithful. And somehow, many of the unfaithful seemed to be doing just fine.

This psalm points out the apparent incongruity between God's plan and human experience. The wicked seemed to be prospering while the righteous were struggling. Other psalmists and prophets take up the same issue, which is not confined to any period or place in history. It's universal. Why does injustice continue? Why do the wicked succeed?

This acrostic psalm takes the long view, with marvelous promises sprinkled throughout. It's filled with enough nuggets of powerful truth to fill our thoughts for a lifetime, but the key theme is this: Living well in the Promised Land requires being in sync with the Promiser. Delight in him, wait for him, be faithful to him, commit to him, and refuse to devote anxious thoughts to the wicked who seem to be prospering (but really aren't in the long view). Fill your heart with trust.

RE-ENVISION THE UNRIGHTEOUS

The anomaly of the unrighteous prospering and the righteous struggling is a chapter in the story of God's people, but it is certainly not the end. Observing life through natural eyes sometimes leads to rash behavior and questions about whether faithfulness is ever rewarded. If it isn't, why not join the unrighteous in their ways?

But God's track record with the righteous is impeccable (v. 25). It's one thing to live comfortably in the land, another to inherit it. No matter how well the ungodly seem to be doing there, eyes of faith see far into the future and know the promised inheritance isn't ultimately theirs. Maintaining faithfulness does pay off. God does give his land (promises) to his people. He establishes those who live out their convictions. He fulfills the desires of those who delight in him.

You know what I long for, Lord; you hear my every sigh.

38:9

David understood the dynamics of guilt. He had committed adultery with Bathsheba and orchestrated the death of her husband (2 Samuel 11). He also ordered a census that resulted in punishment and seventy thousand deaths (2 Samuel 24:1-17). In each case he repented—eventually—but he knew what it meant to be weighed down with shame.

This psalm reflects a common human experience. It's a lament, a plea, and a confession that directly ties suffering to sin. Sin isn't always the source of suffering, of course, but the psalmist is convinced that in this case it is. He's facing the consequences of his own mistakes, and there are physical manifestations of it. He is in emotional, physical, and spiritual pain and knows only one source of help.

That explains the transparency of this psalm. There is no hiding from God. Yes, a rebuke and discipline are deserved (Psalm 38:1); yes, the psalmist is "on the verge of collapse" (v. 17); and yes, he is deeply sorry for what he did (v. 18). But he still sees God as his savior (v. 22). Therefore, he waits (v. 15).

RE-ENVISION YOUR GUILT

Both the righteous and the wicked sin. The difference is that the righteous are painfully aware of it. In that pain, natural eyes see a God who seeks only to punish, discipline, correct, and even withhold blessing. Any mental picture resembling that description results in ongoing guilt, insecurity, doubt, and pessimism in prayer. But Spirit-opened eyes see something different: a God who has long known everything about you, even before you were born, and still chose to pursue you. He had already accounted for your sin and compensated for it before you ever committed it, and even so, he went ahead with his plans for you.

The impulse of the guilty is to run from God at the times when we need him most. Reject that impulse. A true vision of him provokes the opposite response—a suffering believer, clinging to faith, ready to run into God's arms of mercy to receive thorough restoration and rest.

LORD, remind me how brief my time on earth will be. Remind me that my days are numbered—how fleeting my life is.

39:4

Most psalms, even those full of brokenness and pain, end with a hopeful outlook. This one does not. The psalmist is silent before God (vv. 1-2, 9), partly to avoid uttering a potentially negative testimony about God before others, but partly because there may not have been much more to say. He admits his own rebellion (v. 8) and knows not to protest God's discipline (v. 9). All he has is his silence and a glimmer of hope (v. 7).

Meanwhile, he reflects on his life and knows how fleeting it is. He even asks for a reminder of its brevity, as if he knows how distorted his perspective is and wants a new one. He is disoriented by whatever illness or trial he is going through, but he is at least aware of his disorientation. At the moment, he has no answers. But he trusts God enough to long for one.

RE-ENVISION REALITY

When we're in pain, our sense of reality is shaken. Even basic truths we know about God's character and our redemption can get twisted. Our own guilt sends our minds searching for all kinds of cause-and-effect explanations, many of them wildly off base. From our perspective under the consequences of personal sin and human fallenness, with human limitations squeezing ever tighter around us, God is obscured.

We may have difficulty seeing a greater reality at such times, but if we have a proper spiritual perspective, we know there is one. In light of the numerous biblical assurances about who God is and the New Testament promises of our direct access to him through Christ, every area of our lives should be gleaming with hope. If some of them aren't, we need a reorientation.

Ask God for this whenever life looks skewed. Look past the lies surrounding your circumstances and ask the God of hope to give you his perspective (Ephesians 1:17-18). Even from the confines of human brokenness and pain, we can enter his throne room (Hebrews 4:16). Let the vastness of his mercy and the certainty of his promises lift up your eyes.

PSALM 40: OUR STORY, HIS STAGE

He has given me a new song to sing, a hymn of praise to our God. Many will see what he has done and be amazed. They will put their trust in the Lord.

40:3

The previous psalm was almost entirely despair. This one begins with deliverance from it. We can't know whether this refers to a victory in battle, recovery from an illness, deliverance from a rebellion or conspiracy, or forgiveness of sin and freedom from guilt and shame. But whatever it was, it filled the psalmist with joy.

The prayer that was answered at the start leads to another prayer later in the psalm. That's how faith often works; our past experience with God gives us faith for future experiences. When he has shown us his miraculous work, we boldly ask him next time we need a miracle. This psalmist was hardly silent about his deliverance. He was soaring on the heights of a rags-to-riches experience.

He was also very aware of the power of his testimony. Many would see, be amazed, and trust in God. While some people observe the world around them and are consumed with anxiety, anger, judgments, bitterness, or some other expression of spiritual angst, the core message of our lives is supposed to be our journeys of faith-filled exploits and our joyful testimonies about them. We demonstrate the life of faith, and others are drawn to faith. That's how we and others come to know him.

RE-ENVISION YOUR VICTORIES

Learn to see your trials and victories not just as yours but also as a stage for God to demonstrate who he is to a larger audience. While faith is deeply personal, it's often more than that. There's a public side to it. That's easier to see in the life of a king like David, but it's true for all of us. Your story is not just yours; it's also ours. It's a testimony that belongs to the body of Christ as a whole. When others hear the songs of victory that fill your heart, many will see him and sing them too.

PSALM 41: A HEART OF COMPASSION

Oh, the joys of those who are kind to the poor! The Lord rescues them when they are in trouble.

41:1

The first psalm of Book 1 began with a beatitude: "Blessed" (or "happy" or "joyful") are those who do not follow ungodly advice (1:1). The last psalm in Book 1 also begins with one. Here the blessing applies to those who give to the poor, or more generally, those who have a heart for the downtrodden, the marginalized, and the hurting. When they see others as God sees them—as beloved people in need—they begin to respond as he does: with generosity and compassion.

The psalmist didn't come by this perspective accidentally. His affliction seems to have sensitized him to the plight of the poor. Though a king could hardly be considered poor, he felt like one of them. He had suffered from guilt, illness, and the taunts and whispers of those who claimed to be friends but gossiped about his demise. Like the poor, he knew what it was like for the better-offs to gloat over his misfortune.

As powerful as God is, he does not lord it over the poor, the sick, the marginalized, and the brokenhearted—as human lords might. He takes no pleasure in our pain. In fact, his values are completely different from the world's. Jesus displayed God's distinct measuring stick in his paradoxes regarding the Kingdom—the great who serve, the last who will be first, the dead who live, the meek who inherit the earth, and the poor who inherit the Kingdom. God always sides with humble souls who know they need him.

RE-ENVISION YOUR VALUE SYSTEM

How do you measure the people around you? If you want your view of them to match God's, you'll first need to recognize how you appear to him. You are astonishingly treasured and valued but also helpless and needy apart from him. Once you know your own desperation, having compassion for those in need comes naturally.

God blesses this tenderness because it aligns with his heart, and he fills our lives with whatever flows out of us (Luke 6:37). See with eyes of compassion, and God's compassion for you will overflow in your times of need.

BOOK 2: PSALMS 42–72

The tone shifts in Book 2. Many of the same conflicts, affirmations of faith, and celebrations of God are still present, and Israel's national enemies still threaten, but the perspective is more assured, more victorious, and more global in scope. Not only is Israel called to worship God; so are all nations.

BACKGROUND

Perhaps this turn toward all nations comes from the international relations of David and Solomon. Both had diplomatic relationships with many foreign kings and traded with them on friendly terms. Solomon had a reputation for marrying their daughters to create alliances. There were times when Solomon had "peace on every side" (1 Kings 5:4; see also 4:24). A well-established kingdom fit securely in the geopolitical landscape during their reigns.

Book 2 also promotes the reign of the messianic King. A frequent use of *Elohim* (a general name for God) rather than *Yahweh* (the more personal name for Israel's God) may reflect the international vision represented in these psalms. This book ends with a prophecy of the glories of God's Kingdom and a prediction that all nations will serve him. The struggle to establish God's Kingdom on earth in Book 1 seems certain to succeed in Book 2. Even in moments of deep distress, hope runs strong.

Whereas David was identified as the author of most psalms in Book 1, other authors often appear in Book 2. The "descendants of Korah"—Temple ministers and musicians who were established by David when the Tabernacle was in Jerusalem—were responsible for Psalms 42–49. A psalm of Asaph, a leader of Temple musicians, follows (Psalm 50). Psalms 51–71 present a second collection of Davidic psalms, and the book ends with a psalm of Solomon. It also concludes with an ancient editor's note that the psalms of David end here (72:20)—though quite a few more psalms attributed to David are to come. Apparently at one point in the history of the Psalms' compilation, Book 2's global vision of messianic rule had a sense of finality to it.

This subcollection of psalms begins with a psalmist panting and thirsting for God and ends with a psalmist thrilled that the whole earth is filled with God's glory. That's the human story in a nutshell, from Genesis 3 to Revelation 22, the before-and-after picture of redeemed humanity. We are broken, needy people ultimately satisfied by a good, compassionate God. Along the way, there's a royal wedding (Psalm 45), deep confession and repentance (Psalm 51), and the lasting victory of a royal son (Psalm 72), intermixed with laments, pleas, deliverances, and joys that are so common throughout the Psalter. Like every book in Psalms, Book 2 captures the ups and downs of life while pointing to its ultimate meaning and fulfillment.

THE BIG PICTURE

Perhaps the best summary of Book 2—and many other sections of the Psalms—is found in 66:5: "Come and see what our God has done, what awesome miracles he performs for people!" That verse captures both the corporate and personal blessings of knowing God. It speaks of his many benefits and supernatural interventions, including forgiveness, deliverance, and victory in battle;

offers an invitation for those who don't know him to come and see who he is; and incorporates a rich theology based in experience. After all, God doesn't give us a textbook on his nature. His Word is filled with stories of encounters with him and revelations of his nature in real life. Scripture itself is an invitation to "come and see," and like the psalmists, we recognize that our only reasonable response is to notice what he has done and rejoice in it.

Nearly every psalm is a testimony to how God reorients our perspective—how we can be focused on this or that problem, stuck in some pit or another, or focused on a small, inward vision until he rescues, restores, and redirects us into his vastly larger purposes and ways. This portion of the Psalms assures us with personally redemptive stories and then lifts our eyes to much greater stories that reach to the ends of the earth. Our own personal gospel ("good news") becomes the gospel for the world, and we get to see ourselves within that vision. Even more, we get to participate in it. The God we encounter in these psalms is the same God we encounter in our lives today, in any of the circumstances we find ourselves in. And he is still focused on the same purpose—fulfilling his design for our lives and his mission to the world.

PSALM 42: A MISUNDERSTOOD LONGING

As the deer longs for streams of water, so I long for you, O God.

42:1

The psalmist's heart was breaking. He no longer led processions into the Temple (v. 4) and felt oppressed by an ungodly nation (43:1; the next psalm is a continuation of this one). His alienation had left him with "only tears for food" (42:3). We can only speculate about the context. Was he in exile in a foreign land, or perhaps in the northern kingdom of Israel after its split with the southern kingdom of Judah, where the Temple was? Was he deprived of Temple celebrations for some other reason? Whatever the case, he was no longer at God's sanctuary to see foreigners being drawn to God. He could hear the taunts of the enemy questioning why his God wasn't even around to hear his pleas (v. 10). This was not how the Kingdom was supposed to be. He longed for a sense of belonging, but even more, he longed for God himself.

Some will think we're naive to depend on God in a crisis. We'll wait for God to answer our prayers, knowing there's often a gap between promise and fulfillment, but others will see the gap as evidence that our faith is misguided. This is an inevitable part of the believer's experience, and it's painful. It intensifies our longing for God to show up.

RE-ENVISION YOUR FEELINGS

Clearly the psalmist thinks he—or more specifically, his soul—sees a false picture. What's his solution? He talks to himself. He instructs his soul, not to convince himself of what isn't true but of what is. He identifies his misplaced emotions and points himself back to reasonable hope and the certainty that he will praise God again in his future.

Some might call this "positive thinking." Scripture portrays it as a return to reality. If we needed any evidence of our ability to reorient our vision, this is it: We can actually tell ourselves what to think, choose the vision we'll focus on, and replace one perspective with another. Our circumstances and enemies try to impose their vision on us, but God tells us the truth. And his vision always fills us with hope.

PSALM 43: THE BIG SHIFT

Send out your light and your truth; let them guide me. Let them lead me to your holy mountain, to the place where you live.

43:3

This psalm begins where the last one left off, suggesting it should be considered part of the same poem. It uses the same language and tone, does not lead with a separate title to distinguish it from what went before, and asks many of the same questions. The psalmist still wonders why his soul is discouraged and his heart is disturbed, and he continues to mourn.

He knows the answers on the surface, of course. He is surrounded by "unjust liars" (v. 1) and feels tossed aside by God (v. 2). So why is he surprised by his discouragement? Wouldn't anybody despair in such circumstances? Not if they know the end of the story, or if they see their current situation through the right lens, or if they are able to dwell at the altar of God (v. 4). As always, perspectives change in God's presence. Circumstances that once looked threatening suddenly appear negligible. Even though they haven't gone away, they pale in comparison to the God above them.

RE-ENVISION THE POWER OF PRAISE

The last two lines of this psalm are the only truly legitimate perspective in any situation: "My Savior and my God!" (v. 5). Resolutely, the psalmist insists on filling his heart with hope and praising God. This is the key to reorienting our perspective according to truth. We might think we're stuck in our troubles and our feelings about them, but we aren't. Choosing to fill our hearts and mouths with praise—*even when it goes against every impulse within us*—can prompt an enormous shift, changing the atmosphere within us and around us. Eventually, faith begins to rise. And ultimately we marvel and rejoice once again in the light and truth of who God is, what he has done for us already, and what he has promised to do in the future.

PSALM 44: GOD THE WARRIOR

Only by your power can we push back our enemies; only in your name can we trample our foes.

44:5

Gideon was hiding from the Midianites when the angel of the Lord called him to take up his true nature as a mighty warrior. Gideon asked out loud what many had been silently wondering: "If the LORD is with us, why has all this happened to us? And where are all the miracles our ancestors told us about? . . . Now the LORD has abandoned us and handed us over to the Midianites" (Judges 6:13).

That's essentially the lament of this psalm, which rehearses God's past victories but wonders why he has now "tossed us aside in dishonor" (Psalm 44:9). God's people had apparently been defeated—in contradiction both to past victories and to the promise of the land (v. 3). The common, knee-jerk human response, often cynically thought but rarely uttered, is to ask God something like, "Why do you sleep?" (v. 23). Still, the psalmist knows God commands victories for his people (v. 4) and will rise up and ransom them—not because they deserve it, not because they prayed all the right things, and not simply because their enemies are evil, but because of his "unfailing love" (v. 26).

RE-ENVISION YOUR SOURCE

When we pray for God's will to be done "on earth as it is in heaven" (Matthew 6:10), we're also praying for other agendas to be defeated. As the psalmist put it, we want God to "trample our foes" (Psalm 44:5). We don't wish misfortune or defeat on people themselves—we're called to bless, not to curse (Romans 12:14)—but we do have a calling to advance God's Kingdom, and his Kingdom has quite a few opponents. In that conflict, we need to know where our power comes from.

Virtually every believer knows the answer: only by his power. We may add our efforts, arguments, programs, and more, but only God can make it happen. We must have his favor, and he is glad to give it to those who depend on him and not on their own devices. He commands glorious victories for those who give glory to him.

PSALM 45: REALMS CONVERGE

Your sons will become kings like their father. You will make them rulers over many lands.

45:16

The psalmist wrote "a lovely poem about the king" (v. 1), and he was probably certain of which king he was writing about. It's a royal psalm, a love poem, and a wedding song on the occasion of the king's marriage. And not only does it address the king himself; it also addresses the bride (vv. 10-15). In historical context, its personal nature and emphasis on honor seem to fit the culture.

But something more is going on here. The psalmist refers to the king as God (v. 6) and blends the temporal throne with the eternal one. His words seem to operate on two levels. In keeping with God's promise to give David an everlasting dynasty (2 Samuel 7:16), the perception of this human king is loaded. God is clearly the King above him and is working through him.

This psalm is therefore about the kingdom and *the* Kingdom—with all God's promises for Israel and God's eternal reign. And it's about the prophesied Son who would descend from this dynasty (2 Samuel 7:8-16). The messianic implications elevate this poem beyond a mere ancient celebration.

RE-ENVISION YOUR DESTINY

In that elevated meaning beyond the poem's cultural context, you have a place in this wedding. You may see yourself as God's servant or a follower of Jesus, but you're also betrothed. The Old Testament king married his bride, but the messianic King beyond him has a bride too (Matthew 25:1-13; Ephesians 5:25-27; Revelation 21:1-4). The king delights in her (Psalm 45:11), she is showered with gifts (v. 12), and she looks glorious (v. 13). It's the ultimate celebration of a royal love and the fulfillment of a royal agenda, with fruitfulness and honor forever (vv. 16-17).

When you grasp how much the Bridegroom delights in you, you begin to see the relationship differently. That vision changes everything. You act like the beloved, trust in the one who loves you, become more fruitful, and live with joy and a sense of purpose. You are fulfilled—and you are increasingly like the King who chose you.

SONGS OF ZION

Mount Zion (or simply Zion) is often used in Psalms as a synonym for Jerusalem or the Temple Mount—God's designated dwelling place and the spiritual center of ancient Israel—or the whole southern kingdom of Judah. It can also serve as a poetic description of God's people or a metaphor for the entirety of God's Kingdom. And Zion is often used as the subject of hymns and odes to God as King.

Many of these poetic expressions are preserved in the Psalms, especially those categorized as "songs of Zion." These would include Psalms 46–48, 76, 84, 87, and 122. Some commentators add Psalms 125–126, 132, and 137. These psalms focus not only on Jerusalem and the Temple but more specifically on the idea of God's "sanctuary"—the place of his presence where his people worship and commune with him. Not surprisingly, several of these songs are also in the collection known as the "Psalms of Ascent," which celebrate pilgrimage to Jerusalem.

But Zion is not only the place of God's presence. It's where he is enthroned, which also happens to be the place where David and his successors were enthroned. Many of the songs of Zion celebrate David's kingship while also assuming that God rules from both heaven and Jerusalem. The sovereign King and his anointed kings share the same center of rule.* Human and divine thrones merge in the godly kings of Israel.

This gives Mount Zion an eternal air and makes it a symbol of a safe, secure, and just society. It also points toward the Messiah who would come centuries after the psalmists wrote. Their hope was for the establishment of God's reign in Jerusalem and the kingdom of Israel. That hope seemed dashed after the destruction of Jerusalem and the end of David's continuous dynasty, but then it was resurrected after the Exile.

By then, Zion had become an idealized vision of God's Kingdom, still associated with Jerusalem but with far-reaching, even global, implications (46:4, 10)—the throne of the King who would be honored by all and whose Kingdom would never end.

* Robertson, *Flow of the Psalms*, 60–61.

Be still, and know that I am God!
I will be honored by every nation.
I will be honored throughout the world.

46:10

We live in tumultuous times. With the rest of the world, we experience turmoil at social and cultural levels. In our personal journeys through life, we experience it in dark seasons and challenging circumstances. We face crises that can be discouraging, oppressive, and sometimes even brutal. Yet, according to Scripture, God is "our refuge and strength, always ready to help in time of trouble" (v. 1)—or, as some translations put it, "a very present help in trouble" (for example, ESV and NKJV).

In this and the next two psalms, God is exalted as Lord above the nations. No matter what forces of nature, human armies, or personal problems are raging, God is over them all and is zealously protecting his people—here, specifically Jerusalem. God's promises are given in the context of a relationship of faith and loving obedience, of course. Some people in Jeremiah's day falsely thought Jerusalem was invincible no matter how its people lived (Jeremiah 7:4-11). Certainly, that wasn't the case. God expects his followers to serve and obey him. But within covenant conditions, God's protection of his people is unassailable.

Now that Jesus has met the covenant conditions for us, all of God's promises are "yes" in him (2 Corinthians 1:20). We can trust him to command storms to be still, just as he did on a raging sea. In contrast to the turmoil in much of this psalm, there's a peaceful river that brings joy to his people (Psalm 46:4)—not literally in Jerusalem, but clearly in the imagery of his Kingdom (Revelation 22:1-2). Whatever battle is raging, whether in heaven or on earth, he is the victor.

RE-ENVISION THE WORLD

Some people may see your stillness in the midst of a crisis and think you're irresponsible. Trust and apathy can look similar from the outside. But those people don't see what you see—that God will tame it all. In him, you're above the fray and free to abandon worry, cease striving, and speak words of peace into the chaos. He may direct you to take action, but never to do so with a spirit of panic or dread. Everything, including your own heart, must bow to the truth that God is God and *will* accomplish his purposes—here, now, and forever.

PSALM 47: EVERYWHERE AND ALWAYS

All the kings of the earth belong to God. He is highly honored everywhere.

47:9

The previous psalm said to be still. This one calls us to break out of our stillness with shouts, clapping, and praise. It celebrates God's defeat of rival nations and the false gods they trusted (vv. 2-3, 6-8). It may have accompanied a ritual enthronement of divine and human kingship over God's people. Those thrones—the dynasty of David and the future Messiah with the reign of the everlasting God—are merged and rule over "all the kings of the earth." In this divine-human kingship, God is "highly honored everywhere."

This is by no means true in our experience, nor was it true anytime in Israel's or Judah's experience. So when might these encouraging words apply? When is this glorious vision made manifest? We can assume it's a picture of ultimate reality (see Philippians 2:9-11; Revelation 11:15), and in that sense it will be obvious to all when the end of the age unfolds. But for now, is it just a distant hope?

Not according to the rest of the psalm. Because God is already enthroned above all nations, he is in the process of subduing them before us and putting the enemies of his Kingdom beneath our feet (v. 3). Today's headlines tell no such story, but the vision of those who write them is limited. We see a bigger battle of spiritual powers and, even while blessing our human enemies, proceed in confidence that the forces of evil are done for.

RE-ENVISION GOD'S REIGN

If you've ever been tempted to see God's reign as narrow in scope (for now) or limited to the future, look beyond the world's assaults on your senses. Jesus has already ascended, we are already seated with him at the right hand of God's throne (see Ephesians 2:6), and he has sent us out with his authority (Matthew 28:18-20). Any Christian living with a defeatist attitude has fallen for a lie. The truth will put praise in our mouths and energy in our steps.

We had heard of the city's glory, but now we have seen it ourselves— the city of the LORD of Heaven's Armies.

48:8

Like other ancient hymns that glorify a king and city, this song of Zion extols the beauty and magnificence of Jerusalem. To an ancient Hebrew, the sight must have been impressive—strategically positioned on a hill, with high walls and strong towers, foreboding enough to put enemies to flight. It was majestic and invincible—just like God.

In fact, this is why the psalmist praises the city so lavishly. It isn't that the city itself is so glorious (though it may have seemed that way), but it is glorious because God dwells there. His presence is the defining characteristic that gives the city its allure (vv. 3, 8). The psalmist does not suggest that God is present *only* in Jerusalem and its Temple but that these are special places of his manifest presence. Just as God's presence filled the Temple when Solomon dedicated it, the divine presence remains among his people.

This vision of God's presence had a very material focus to ancient eyes, but the new covenant expands it beyond place and time. God now dwells within his people, not just among them, and we are in every corner of the world. Wherever his "city" is, it should be like him—secure, impressive, impervious to enemies, glorious enough for the whole earth to rejoice. We have become the holy habitation and are called to live like it.

RE-ENVISION YOUR BEAUTY AND STRENGTH

This has huge implications for followers of Jesus who are filled with God's Spirit. If we see ourselves merely as believers or followers or sinners saved by grace—all of which are true, but only starting points—we will live with low expectations and limited growth. But if we see ourselves as glorious temples of the Most High God, we step into a fuller vision, a greater glory, and a more joyous, fruitful life. With our feet on unshakable ground and our eyes on an invincible King, we stand as towers he has strengthened and made beautiful with his presence.

As for me, God will redeem my life. He will snatch me from the power of the grave.

49:15

The previous four psalms have emphasized God as King and the city of Jerusalem as the place of his presence for his people. That's a great vision for current and future battles, but the struggles of daily life play out more slowly on a much smaller scale. What does the victorious God have for us in our routine lives? Wisdom.

This psalm, similar in tone to Proverbs and Ecclesiastes (and summed up well in Jeremiah 9:23-24), appeals to all people everywhere to hear God's wisdom, especially with regard to wealth. Death comes to all, regardless of status or riches, even to those who trust their own wisdom—and it's futile to live without that awareness. This psalm again raises the question of why the ungodly prosper and the righteous struggle, pointing out that the ungodly only *appear* to prosper—for now. If everyone dies with empty pockets and purses, the story of our lives must be assessed by other criteria. Anyone who boasts in riches is boasting in something very transitory—just like their lives.

RE-ENVISION YOUR TREASURES

Rich fools will die like animals, the psalmist says. They have no vision beyond their limited time. The remedy, he urges, is to spend your life looking beyond earthly riches, refusing to base your success on what is superficial. What appears to be prosperity is not. There will come a day for everyone when true treasures are made perfectly clear, and those who did not seek them will invariably be filled with regret.

The wise bring the clarity of that moment into today. They can anticipate their vision at the end of life and live from it now—without regret. They see through the luster of momentary riches and invest themselves instead in true riches that last beyond the grave, never having to fear losing what they treasure (see Matthew 6:19-21).

PSALM 50: SACRIFICES OF THE HEART

Make thankfulness your sacrifice to God, and keep the vows you made to the Most High. Then call on me when you are in trouble, and I will rescue you, and you will give me glory.

50:14-15

God judges human hearts. He sees into the depths of every one of them and draws conclusions about which ways they lean. What is he looking for? First, whether they have embraced his covenant by entering into a relationship with him; and second, how they respond to that relationship.

The psalmist describes two approaches to God and life: one of sacrifices and appeasement, the other of genuine affection and honor. The former is all about playing the game—giving God his due, jumping through whatever hoops they think he has placed before them—and the latter is about authentic connection. God bases his judgments on whether keeping the covenant of faith is lip service or sincere love. He wants his people to incline their hearts toward him and genuinely interact with him—primarily through gratitude and commitment.

The people surrounding Israel were accustomed to worshiping gods who were seen as dependent on sacrifices that they would consume for sustenance. God distinguished himself from such practices. He valued the faith and devotion behind sacrifices, and his law prescribed many offerings because of what they symbolized. But depending on them for nourishment? Not Israel's God. Rituals may be an expression of devotion to God, but they are never the substance of it. Without true faith, these sacrifices are empty and even offensive. So the psalmist warned God's people to worship with gratitude and *live out* their praises before him.

RE-ENVISION SACRIFICES

Jesus told his followers to "take up your cross, and follow me" (Matthew 16:24), and Paul urged us to present ourselves to God as living sacrifices (Romans 12:1). We read these verses with an assumption that sacrifices involve deprivation and hardship. Often they do, but there's a more satisfying offering we should place on the altar before God: our thankfulness and commitment, along with our praises and peace. We honor him when we let go of stress, fear, and discouragement and embrace the joy of his Kingdom instead. Nothing reflects his nature better than his people delighting in him.

Create in me a clean heart, O God. Renew a loyal spirit within me.

51:10

At great risk to his position (and perhaps his life), Nathan the prophet confronted David for committing adultery with Bathsheba and arranging her husband's death (2 Samuel 12). Once David's eyes were opened to his sin, he repented immediately and deeply. The prayer in this psalm is his agonizing confession and plea for mercy.

David had lost his shalom—the fullness, wholeness, and peace of life with God—and wanted it back. He longed to sense the Holy Spirit again and live as joyfully and freely as he once did. Sin interrupted the blessings of that relationship; it always complicates life and leaves behind all kinds of scars and confusion. And David knew God well enough to know restoration was possible—that God would not despise "a broken and repentant heart" (Psalm 51:17).

The way this prayer is written, it could apply to any situation in which repentance is appropriate. It captures the essence of our relationship with God, and even though this was written centuries before the sacrifice of Jesus to pay for our sins, it assumes the same willingness of God to cancel our sins and restore us to righteousness. Not only does he forgive our sins; he helps clean up the mess. Consequences may linger, but God's restoration puts us in sync with him, undoes sin's lasting effects, and makes life flow again.

RE-ENVISION YOUR LOSSES

You've probably experienced the gaping wounds and huge sense of loss left by missing God's best due to your sin. The good news is that God does not abandon us; he is particularly drawn to the brokenhearted. You no longer need to view your losses and regrets as irrevocable setbacks. He loves to restore the years the locusts have eaten (Joel 2:25, ESV).

Imagine living with the freedom of a heart uncluttered by sin, guilt, and shame, and let that vision drive you to God with prayers for healing and restoration. There is no sin he is unwilling to forgive when you come to him in repentance with a desire to experience him fully again.

I am like an olive tree,
thriving in the house of God.
I will always trust in God's unfailing love.

52:8

Doeg the Edomite told Saul where David had been and which priests had helped him. And when Saul's men refused to take vengeance on the priests, Doeg killed all eighty-five of the priests—plus all their wives, children, and livestock (1 Samuel 21:7; 22:6-23). David must have felt awful to have been the catalyst for such a slaughter; he could have even questioned whether his anointing as future king was still valid. Truly Doeg's tongue cut like a razor (Psalm 52:2).

But David refused to bear any guilt for this catastrophe and, by the time of this psalm, emphasized God's promised vengeance against those who plot evil. David knew that, in keeping with God's stated rejection of those who rejected the covenant—which the Edomite had done at multiple levels—Doeg, as a murderer, would be uprooted from the land. And David knew he himself would not. In fact, he would remain like an olive tree—wonderfully fruitful and so deeply rooted that even near destruction could not keep him from thriving (v. 8).

David remarkably pledged to praise God forever "for what you have done" (v. 9)—although it had not yet been done. Though Doeg (and similar evildoers) had not yet been uprooted, their eventual destruction was certain. David trusted God's purposes enough to know they were assured.

RE-ENVISION YOUR SECURITY

In the previous psalm, David was the evildoer. In this one, his adversary was. Why would he expect different treatment? Because, as the previous psalm shows, David had a repentant heart, grief over his sin, and an awareness of his wrongdoing and the trouble it caused. He could therefore rest in God's forgiveness and expect judgment against the unrepentant.

Insecure believers have trouble seeing the difference between themselves and the unrepentant and often envision themselves as reeds in the wind. But you're an olive tree. No matter how far you're cut back, you'll just keep growing. You're rooted in God's faithfulness and will always be refreshed by the waters of his unfailing love.

When God restores his people, Jacob will shout with joy, and Israel will rejoice.

53:6

Whether intended or not, this psalm adds emphasis to the condemnation of Doeg in the previous psalm. He serves as at least one illustration of the psalm's subject—those who reject God. Almost identical to Psalm 14, this psalm also calls the atheist a fool (v. 1). But here the psalmist uses the more generic word for God (*Elohim*) throughout rather than his covenant name (*Yahweh*)—possibly to apply these words to non-Israelites. Like the foreigner Doeg, who showed no conscience or morality in what he did, such fools "eat up" God's people and wouldn't think of praying to him (v. 4). Clearly there is a correlation between those who reject God and those who reject his loved ones.

This psalm also differs from Psalm 14 in one other respect. The earlier psalm tells those who reject God that he will take care of the oppressed. This one tells them he scatters the bones of those who come against his people (v. 5). In either case, he defends those who love him. Those who don't love him have chosen his rejection instead.

RE-ENVISION POWER

Power struggles between ancient Israelites and their enemies, while historically interesting, may not seem very relevant to us today. But when we realize that they illustrate much larger battles playing out in the world and in realms we cannot see with natural eyes, they take on greater meaning. Those who love God will always find refuge in him. Those who don't will have much less power than they think.

Which battle are you involved in? Do you primarily see the power struggle playing out in the politics and institutions of this world? Or do you see the one playing out in heavenly realms, behind the scenes, where a different narrative is taking place that ultimately ends with the defeat and shame of evildoers? Far too many Christians get lost in the chaos of worldly struggles; those with clearer vision go to battle with unearthly weapons to influence the unseen spiritual war. Step into the story God is writing and invest your energy in the struggle that matters most.

May the evil plans of my enemies be turned against them. Do as you promised and put an end to them.

54:5

Do as you promised. There is no more certain prayer, yet we often inject a lot of uncertainty into it. The psalmist prayed it in the midst of a crisis, and even though he was sure God would deliver him, he still seemed alarmed. We're told the context: The Ziphites were betraying David to Saul (1 Samuel 23:19-20; 26:1-4). This is the first in a series of psalms that identify an enemy of David and express either the confidence that God will bring the victory or the gratitude that he has already done so. David was very familiar with God doing as he promised.

This psalm could have been used by any successor king, in a variety of situations—the attacks of foreign armies, a judicial trial with false accusers, a coup attempt, or virtually any other crisis. And it isn't only applicable in royal predicaments; it fits any situation that feels oppressive, threatening, unjust, or otherwise troubling. God's promises apply to everyone who loves and trusts him. We can pray those promises broadly.

RE-ENVISION YOUR ENEMY

It's perhaps more positive to focus on deliverance and praising God for how he has rescued (or will rescue) us, themes clearly present here, but a prayer against enemies is one of the focal points of this psalm. We aren't to wish evil against humans—our struggle is not against them (Ephesians 6:12; see also 2 Corinthians 10:3-5), and we are called to bless, not to curse (Romans 12:14)—but we are fighting an invisible war against forces of darkness. We can rest on God's promise that no weapon formed against us will prosper (Isaiah 54:17, NKJV), as well as Jesus' victory on the cross, which completely flipped the script on the enemy and stripped him of all power and authority against us. There's nothing wrong with praying that all the enemy's schemes will backfire and envisioning a resounding defeat for all of them. And no prayer for victory in such battles is a mere wish. It's a prayer of certainty that God will deliver us from our enemies and do exactly as he promised.

PSALM 55: WHERE BURDENS BELONG

Give your burdens to the LORD, and he will take care of you. He will not permit the godly to slip and fall.

55:22

Multiple enemies appear in this psalm, but the one at the center is the most painful—a former companion who betrayed the psalmist (vv. 12-14, 20-21). In another psalm, David scoffed at the mere idea that he might fly away like a bird to safety (11:1). Here he wishes he could (55:6-7)—an impulse most of us have felt in dark or intense times. He expresses genuine, heart-pounding fear (vv. 4-5). He is in one of those seasons in which occasional or even frequent prayer is not enough. He is crying out constantly (v. 17).

Perhaps the most familiar line from this psalm is verse 22, quoted in 1 Peter 5:7. Here the psalmist turns away from his own crisis and prayers to encourage others to depend on the Lord for all their cares too. It's reliable advice, if difficult to follow. Our impulse is to carry the weight of our worries—something God never called us to do.

RE-ENVISION YOUR RESPONSIBILITIES

Who do you see as the carrier of your burdens? If you've said, thought, or acted like you have the weight of the world on your shoulders, it's you. And you were never meant to do that.

You were designed to carry burdens only as long as it takes to present them to God in prayer—with faith and gratitude that he will answer. Much of your life involves the dynamic of encountering burdens and then casting them onto him. As an intercessor, you are positioned to receive these troubles and send them away instantly. You're their transmitter, not their bearer. If you hang on to them, you've stepped out of your original design.

That may seem irresponsible, but does it make more sense for you to carry the weight of huge problems in your finite strength or put them into his infinitely strong hands? The more responsible course should be obvious. You can—and should—trust him with them. He has promised to handle them well.

You have rescued me from death; you have kept my feet from slipping. So now I can walk in your presence, O God, in your life-giving light.

56:13

The occasion for this psalm of David was when "the Philistines seized him in Gath." David spent time in Gath twice (1 Samuel 21:10-15; 27:1–28:2), in both cases by his own choice to avoid the wrath of Saul. But even voluntary exile in enemy territory was traumatizing, and David felt harassed, threatened, and sad. He poured his heart out to the God who cared so deeply that he would collect all David's tears in a bottle (Psalm 56:8).

Such psalms written in the midst of danger contain common themes. In addition to lament, there's often a prayer and almost always some affirmation that God will come through. Here the affirmation comes in praise (three times) for what God has promised and a statement that "mere mortals" had no power over David (vv. 4, 10-11).

But this psalm also contains another common theme: a promise to fulfill vows to the Lord. Plenty of psalms speak of vows (see, for example, 22:25; 50:14; 61:8; 65:1; 66:13-14; 116:18). These vows are often accompanied with sacrifices of praise and gratitude. In return for some great work God has done in a time of crisis, the psalmist makes a commitment to do some act of service to God. The cynic would see it as dealmaking—"If you get me out of this mess . . ." But the psalmist almost always sees it as heartfelt thanks.

RE-ENVISION YOUR NEW LIFE

Some people focus on what God hasn't done for them yet and grow bitter, but that inward vision represents a step back into the darkness after having seen the light. The story of this psalm and of every redeemed life is a dramatic rescue and an entirely new beginning of walking in the "life-giving light" of his presence. Live as someone who owes your whole life to the Rescuer. Praise him for what he has promised (v. 10-11). Through new eyes, look with wonder at everything. Celebrate your new beginning. The reason he collected your tears was to turn them to joy.

I cry out to God Most High, to God who will fulfill his purpose for me.

57:2

Think of the questions David could have had as he fled from Saul and hid in a cave (1 Samuel 22:1): *Did I miss God's purpose? Forfeit his calling because of some sin? Not have enough faith? Maybe I missed the window of opportunity, and now he's changed his mind?* We may wrestle intensely with such questions when we consider apparent delays in God's promises and purposes because we know these delays aren't simply "fate" or "destiny." But we must remember that they are an invitation, a calling that requires a response. And unless that response is outright rebellion, we can trust his purposes and expect him to fulfill them.

David cried out to God not because he wanted to persuade God to fulfill his purposes but because he already knew God would. Most of us haven't been hunted like wild prey, but we have faced vicious situations that terrorized our hearts and made us feel like running and hiding in a cave. Like David, we can "plead God's promises" in full confidence. And, like David, we can go ahead and praise God for the outcome (Psalm 57:7). What he has said is reality, whether we've gotten to it on the timeline yet or not.

RE-ENVISION GOD'S PROMISES

To some, God's promises and purposes are mere possibilities. They are outcomes we might hope for, but they aren't set in stone; we'll have to wait and see how things play out. But eyes of faith envision God's promises as something much more concrete. They are a done deal, money in the bank, an irrevocable oath we can rest in completely.

When we see God's promises and purposes this way, we can endure a lot. We also change the way we pray. Instead of trying to twist God's arm to do something he might be reluctant to do, we ask him instead to do what he said. We put behind us every "maybe so" and "wait and see." Certain that his "faithfulness reaches to the clouds" (v. 10), we can rest confidently on whatever he has said—even if we're hiding in a cave.

IMPRECATORY PSALMS

It isn't difficult to find harsh statements in the Psalms. Out of the raw emotions of the psalmists—some of them in extraordinarily stressful situations—flow curses against the enemies responsible for their pain. Lament psalms that contain curses are known as "imprecatory psalms" because they pronounce imprecations (curses) on adversaries. These include Psalms 35, 55, 58–59, 69, 79, 109, and 137. This is a natural human response to evil, but Scripture repeatedly calls us to rise above our natural inclinations. New creations, supernaturally reborn by God's Spirit, strive for a higher standard than what we see in some biblical characters.

That doesn't mean the psalms aren't inspired, though. Through the psalmists, God's Spirit has preserved true expressions of the human condition, many of which rightly judge evil and those who commit it. Sometimes these curses line up with God's previously revealed Word—the curses found in Leviticus 26 and Deuteronomy 28, for example. So these statements of raw emotion are "true" in the sense that they are biblical. But they also point to deeper biblical truths.

We are familiar with this idea of "true" and "truer" from the teaching of Jesus. For example, "an eye for an eye" and "a tooth for a tooth" is biblical (Exodus 21:24), but Jesus pointed to what we might call a higher or deeper truth to supersede the retaliatory principle: turning the other cheek (Matthew 5:38-42). Our judgment against evil is right. Our love for evildoers is even better.

We must view the curses of the psalms as consistent with the revelation the psalmists were given at that time, but we can also recognize that we have been given a greater revelation. God will judge evil in time; that's his prerogative, and his heart is even more opposed to evil than ours. He also imparts a divine sense of truth and justice to us, which may provoke a harsh reaction to the evil we see. Yet we are told to bless, not curse (Romans 12:14), and we see the redemptive story from this side of the cross. "Mercy triumphs over judgment" (James 2:12-13, ESV), even in a righteously indignant heart.

PSALM 58: WHEN JUSTICE COMES

At last everyone will say, "There truly is a reward for those who live for God; surely there is a God who judges justly here on earth."

58:11

Some people seem shocked at injustice, as if it's some sort of novelty. But it has been here since nearly the beginning. People in power take advantage of the powerless; fallen human nature seeks self-interest over the common good; and virtually every society has its share of greased palms, weighted scales, false accusations, and biased law enforcement. Why would we be surprised? This is what sin does to a rebellious planet.

The psalmist writes of a specific injustice, but his words apply in many situations. Though his curses against enemies come from an understandable human impulse—the Psalms are filled with raw emotion—we've been given a better way (Matthew 5:43-48). The people of ancient Israel saw their enemies as very real, in-the-flesh threats, but we know our battle is not against flesh and blood (Ephesians 6:12). In fact, the word translated "rulers" in Psalm 58:1 may actually refer to "gods," and the words of this psalm could easily apply to our conflict with spiritual powers of darkness. Even so, we have enough experience with human injustice to long for "a God who judges justly here on earth."

RE-ENVISION JUSTICE

People who trust in power and money act like they run the world, but they don't see the whole picture. We take comfort in the fact that they will one day envy God's most humble followers—the ones they used to trample on—as inheritors of the earth. Their power and wealth carry no currency in the Kingdom of God.

But for now, we again have a choice. We can focus on how well the wicked are doing or on how certain God's promises are. Whichever of those fills our vision will largely determine our mood, our level of faith, and even our outcomes. One fills us with despair, the other with faith—the true currency of God's Kingdom. And faith will be rewarded in ways the unjust will never know.

PSALM 59: A MORNING SONG

As for me, I will sing about your power. Each morning I will sing with joy about your unfailing love. For you have been my refuge, a place of safety when I am in distress.

59:16

David was serving faithfully in Saul's court and was married to Saul's daughter Michal, but because the king had become increasingly paranoid about David's popularity, David's life was in danger. In fact, Saul posted guards at David's house one night for them to kill him in the morning, and only through Michal's intervention did David escape through a window (1 Samuel 19:11-17). This psalm corresponds to that occasion.

But the psalm goes beyond this personal threat to David's life. It refers to "hostile nations" (Psalm 59:5, 8) and appeals to God to deal with them (v. 5), reflecting a dynamic larger than the immediate situation. This psalm's pleas can apply to any situation of desperate need—when we feel besieged, targeted, threatened, oppressed, or abused. Whether the crisis is personal or corporate, verbal or physical, major or minor, these words express our longing for refuge.

RE-ENVISION YOUR OUTLOOK

As usual, the psalmist makes a choice not to focus on the chaos but to sing about God's power. He isn't singing only with hope; he's also singing with joy. He could look at how precarious his situation is *or* talk about how sure God's refuge is. He could dwell on his danger *or* rest in his safety. Natural eyes would see nothing but peril here. But supernatural eyes—Spirit-inspired eyes of faith—see peace. Sure, there might be turbulence surrounding the peace, but it's an insignificant turbulence compared to the overwhelming power of God.

The eyes of the soul are very persuasive. They dictate our entire outlook, which then dictates what we think, say, and do, which in turn affects what we receive from God and experience in the world. When the eyes of our soul convince us each morning to "sing with joy about [God's] unfailing love," even in a crisis, we've set the course, not just of our day but of our lives, securely under the watch of our Father.

PSALM 60: REPAIRING THE WORLD

With God's help we will do mighty things, for he will trample down our foes.

60:12

The heading of this psalm gives it a context of battles (perhaps 2 Samuel 8:3-6; 10:6-19). It also tells us this psalm is "useful for teaching"—a hint at how it might have been used in Israel's history, not only for worship but also for instruction. The first verse tells us the battles have not gone well, suggesting that God has rejected his people and withdrawn his favor—a catastrophic turn of events for a nation that knew its very existence depended on God's power.

Even so, God had promised "by his holiness" (or "in his sanctuary," Psalm 60:6) that he would divide up nations as inheritances for his people, and the psalmist took his word for it. He followed up with a geographic tour of foreign (or foreign-influenced) places in and around the kingdom of Israel—Shechem, Succoth, Gilead, Manasseh, Ephraim, Moab, Edom, and Philistia. Some were in the fold (technically); most were not. Yet even from the start, the psalmist appeals to the divine agenda: to restore (v. 1), to repair ("seal the cracks," v. 2), and to rescue (v. 5). Even when everything appeared contrary to the promise, the psalmist still trusted the promise.

RE-ENVISION YOUR MISSION

The divine agenda to restore, repair, and rescue makes for a great vision of our role in the world as believers. It fits the Jewish concept of *tikkun olam*—"repairing the world"—and reflects the coming Kingdom. We're called to demonstrate who God is. Or, as Daniel put it, "The people who know their God shall be strong, and carry out great exploits" (Daniel 11:32, NKJV). No matter how defeated you feel in a situation, whatever vulnerable position you may be in, Scripture gives you an entirely different vision. You are called to do "mighty things" to restore, repair, and rescue in every battle you face.

PSALM 61: THE HIGHER ROCK

From the ends of the earth, I cry to you for help when my heart is overwhelmed. Lead me to the towering rock of safety.

61:2

The psalmist was far from home. He cried out "from the ends of the earth" and prayed for the refuge of "the towering rock of safety"—or, as other translations put it, "the rock that is higher than I" (v. 2, NKJV). This is the first of four psalms that cry out for the establishment of God's Kingdom; they are followed by four that affirm the divine King.* As is so often the case, circumstances are tumultuous, and the only hope for peace is the God who authors it. The psalmist is searching for shalom from its only real source.

Though this is called a "psalm of David," it contains a section that is a prayer for the king. Unless David prayed for himself in the third person, it must be a psalm in David's tradition, or a psalm about him, or the work of one of his successors claiming the weight of his name. In any case, it's the cry of someone in a highly undesirable situation. The psalmist wants to somehow live in the fortress of God while also doing business in the open battlefield. It's a seemingly impossible dilemma, yet it feels strangely familiar.

RE-ENVISION YOUR VULNERABILITY

We don't have to be oppressed by the world, but we do have to live in it. We naturally feel vulnerable to "the enemy"—Satan, or more generally his kingdom

* Robertson, *Flow of the Psalms*, 111.

of darkness—yet we long for the strong tower that stands against him. We find ourselves in very undesirable situations at times, yet we don't face them alone. The rock that is higher than we are is always there for our refuge.

What does it look like to live in a safe fortress—the ultimate rock of safety? The way you envision yourself in the midst of a crisis says a lot about how you will come out of it. Reject any image of your vulnerability to the kingdom of darkness; instead see yourself as ultimately invincible. By yourself, you aren't invincible at all. But in him, nothing can truly harm you.

PSALM 62: WAITING ON GOD

I wait quietly before God,
for my victory comes from him.

62:1

Many were trying to shake and topple the psalmist, yet he clung to the truth that God was his rock—a fortress that made him unshakable. But the fact that he has had to repeatedly say so tells us something about the dynamics of resistance. When the threats of life are swirling around us, whenever we feel besieged or broken, when we just can't seem to catch a break, the example of the psalmist is clear: We are to declare emphatically and repeatedly that God is the source of our security, protection, victory, and honor. It's as if David is insistently speaking to his own soul: "Keep looking at him, keep looking at him. . . ."

Paul quoted verse 12—"Surely you repay all people according to what they have done"—in Romans 2:6 to warn the sinful of God's judgment, but the psalmist wrote it to urge patience. God will vindicate his people in time, and he will give them victories along the way. But vindication and victory don't always come on our schedule. Waiting on him is one of the hardest things to do, especially as circumstances evolve and he seems slow to act. Yet that's the way of faith and the only way to see how he unfolds things in the end.

RE-ENVISION YOUR DECLARATION

In the midst of turmoil, perspectives get skewed. Adversaries see God's people as vulnerable—"a broken-down wall or a tottering fence" (Psalm 62:3). If David went by appearances, he would come to the same conclusion. Would he then be delivered? If faith and words figure into our outcomes, perhaps not. By agreeing with the enemies' perspective, David might end up experiencing the tragic consequences of his perceived vulnerability. Seeing things accurately is not just about encouragement in a tough time. It may literally affect the outcome.

This psalm reorients perspectives. David was not actually in a vulnerable position, but his attackers were (v. 9). And this vision, this declaration of faith, may have made all the difference.

PSALM 63: VISIONS IN THE NIGHT

Your unfailing love is better than life itself. . . . You satisfy me more than the richest feast.

63:3, 5

David was "in the wilderness of Judah," perhaps in flight from Saul or his own son Absalom. At one level, this psalm is a straightforward lament about that dreadful time, and as he so often did, David turned his thoughts away from his enemies' threats and filled his mind instead with expectations of deliverance and declarations of praise. He lifted his hands in prayer (v. 4), meditated on God throughout the night (v. 6), and sang for joy under God's care (v. 7). The movie screen of his mind was playing scenes not of capture and defeat but of God's good promises and intentions toward him.

On another level, this psalm could easily have been prayed by Jesus during his temptation in the wilderness—the same wilderness David wrote from. Jesus also clung to the Father spiritually, emotionally, and physically in that "parched and weary land" (v. 1), and he likewise knew the fate of his enemies: Those plotting against him would come to ruin in the depths of the earth and the liar would be silenced (vv. 9, 11). Jesus, too, entertained no visions of defeat, only of ultimate victory.

RE-ENVISION YOUR WORST-CASE SCENARIOS

That's hard to do in the quiet, dark moments of our lives. Most of us have experienced how the night brings out our most alarming, anxiety-inducing thoughts. Worst-case scenarios seem so real when we're lying awake with worry. But this is exactly when it's most crucial to turn our thoughts to who God is, which David willed himself to do (v. 6). We do have choices. Instead of fixating on the bad things that could happen, why not fixate instead on the good? Considering God's nature and his promises, we can expect "the richest feast" even in the desert—and keeping this focus is a far more satisfying way to live.

PSALM 64: FLIPPING THE SCRIPT

Then everyone will be afraid; they will proclaim the mighty acts of God and realize all the amazing things he does.

64:9

The book of Esther details a heinous plot against the Jews scattered throughout Persia by an evil schemer named Haman. Through surprising (and almost comic) twists and turns, God completely reversed the plot so that Mordecai, Haman's Jewish nemesis, was exalted and Haman was destroyed by his own devices. God miraculously turned the tables on the enemy and produced a great victory for his people.

Centuries earlier, this psalm described the same dynamic. It could easily function as a summary preview of Esther. But it's also a familiar dynamic in world history: God's faithful people being targeted by the unfaithful (and some who hypocritically claim to be on God's side), yet God preserving his people against all human odds. Eventually, the godly who were hunted become the victorious, while the hunter falls into his own trap.

Although at first glance it might sound appealing to watch our enemies suffer, we would be wise to take a different perspective. Jesus told us to love our enemies and bless those who persecute us (Matthew 5:43-45), and even though God does eventually judge those who persist in evil, he also calls them to himself in repentance (and sends us out to do the same). Jesus didn't come to judge the world but to save it (John 3:17). That's the mission we're on in this age.

RE-ENVISION YOUR ADVERSARIES

Your spiritual adversary is certainly worthy of the attitudes expressed in this psalm, and God will give the kind of victory over his schemes that the psalmist calls for here. But your human adversaries have their own wounded hearts. They are broken souls unknowingly acting out their own pain and distorted understanding. God can flip the script in their lives, too, and he often does so when his people lay down their judgments, envision their enemies' rescue, love them, and pray them into the Kingdom. No military victory is greater, no testimony clearer in demonstrating "all the amazing things" God does.

You faithfully answer our prayers with awesome deeds, O God our savior.

65:5

God brings order and fruitfulness out of chaos. That's what he did in creation, in delivering his people out of Egypt and through the wilderness into the Land of Promise, and in calming storms of many kinds. And he still does it in speaking his shalom into our lives today. He cares for the earth and longs to give his people an abundant harvest—materially, spiritually, relationally, and more.

After the long strings of laments found in the preceding psalms and a few verses of confession, gratitude, and worship to open this psalm, the theme shifts to abundance. It's the first of four consecutive psalms that celebrate God's (and the messianic King's) reign over all the earth, including distant nations that are destined to praise him but don't realize it yet. At individual, corporate, and even global levels, it celebrates a restored relationship with God. And, in keeping with covenant promises (Leviticus 26:3-5; Deuteronomy 28:1-6), it recognizes the blessing of fruitful land for the righteous.

Clearly this material focus has spiritual applications. The river of God with "plenty of water" (Psalm 65:9) is a loaded metaphor with many implications for those of us who long for the living water of his Spirit to flow increasingly out of us. While many believers assume they will receive only a modest portion, his paths "overflow with abundance" (v. 11). God wants our hearts and lives to be full.

RE-ENVISION ABUNDANCE

This psalm envisions God as someone who wants to bless his people, not only with the rich spiritual blessings he has given us (Ephesians 1:3) but also with pleasant experiences and ample provision. The health-and-wealth gospel leans to an unhealthy extreme on this issue, but many Christians have leaned too far in the other direction. Few see how eager God is to pour his abundance into our lives (2 Corinthians 9:6-15)—not for our mere gratification but for the growth of the Kingdom, for us to be generous with others, and so that we can enjoy his good gifts (see 1 Timothy 6:17). Fill your mind and heart with visions of the river of God, brimming with "plenty of water" (Psalm 65:9), and expect it to flow abundantly into your life—spiritually, physically, emotionally, relationally, and in every other way it can flow.

PSALM 66: THE POWER OF A TESTIMONY

Sing about the glory of his name! Tell the world how glorious he is.

66:2

The invitation of this psalm is to "come and see what our God has done" (v. 5), and from there it rehearses many key events in Israel's history—slavery in Egypt, deliverance through the Red Sea, entrance into the Promised Land. This is Israel's testimony, but the psalm reaches further than that. It's global in scope. What God has done for the Israelites is meant to be a testimony to everyone. Not only is Israel called to shout for joy in their God; all the earth should too.

God's work in the lives of his people is bigger than helping them out or showing them his goodness. It's a demonstration of his nature, for us and others to see. Not all his works are meant to be public—his ministry to us is often deeply personal. But many of his works are intended to showcase his glory, and they become a stage for revealing who he is. As bearers of irrefutable personal testimonies (not that people won't refute them, but they will have no evidence for doing so), we carry the evidence of God within us.

RE-ENVISION YOUR PLACE IN THE WORLD

Amid culture wars and international conflict, we need to remember that God has not called us to be a generation of arguers. Neither has he called us to be known for our laments. He is establishing us as a generation of joyful declarers—people who are confident in who he is, believers who remain unrattled in the face of twisted philosophies and accusations. To the degree we see ourselves as evidence of God's goodness and power, we will not get sucked into fruitless arguments. We will recognize that our only calling is to live out the truth—first and foremost, the truth about God and what he has done. When God's people live supernatural, unexplainable lives, the world's reasonings and accusations prove empty. And despite the chaos all around us, many will see just how glorious he is.

PSALM 67: A FRUITFUL MISSION

May the nations praise you, O God.
Yes, may all the nations praise you.
Then the earth will yield its harvests,
and God, our God, will richly bless us.

67:5-6

In the eyes of the ancient Israelites, faithfulness to the covenant resulted in good harvests and numerous other blessings. This was not a fabrication of the Hebrew mind; God himself had said so in outlining the blessings and curses of the covenant (Leviticus 26; Deuteronomy 28). This psalm celebrates the faithfulness of the people and the harvests that result. And it expands that vision to "all the nations."

It isn't difficult to spiritualize this vision as a prophecy pointing to the great commission and a continuing harvest of souls. God is at work everywhere in the world—preparing hearts, sending his people, desiring to bless and to save. We can be sure that Jesus did not send his disciples out into the world on a mission of futility. His ultimate purpose is to restore the world under the Messiah's reign.

RE-ENVISION HISTORY

Many Christians hold to a rather depressing eschatology, envisioning history as headed toward disaster—increasing conflict, dwindling numbers of believers, shrinking influence of the church, and the apparent rule of ungodly forces until Jesus returns. Elements of that scenario are clear in Scripture, but so are elements of the Kingdom coming and victories being won. Our entire outlook and labor for the Lord are affected by our view of what's ahead.

What is God really doing in the world? Yes, there's a spiritual battle, but there's also his ever-growing Kingdom and his ultimate purpose—for his glory to cover the earth. And since his glory is in his people (John 17:22), that means his people will cover the earth. That's a very encouraging vision. It tells us that there will be greater unveilings of who he is to those who do not know him and that sooner or later, all the nations will in fact praise him, just as the psalmist said.

PSALM 68: LIVING THE VICTORY

Blessed be the Lord, who daily loads us with benefits, the God of our salvation!

68:19, NKJV

In highly symbolic language, the psalmist writes that "the Lord came from Mount Sinai into his sanctuary" (v. 17), leading a procession of defeated captives and bearing the spoils of battle. It's a dramatic picture of a common event—a victorious king humiliating his enemies by parading their defeat for all to see. In this case, the victorious King is God, the warrior who wins battles for his people, not only in the past but also in the future (vv. 21-23, 28). The kings of the earth will bring tribute to God's Temple (v. 29), whether literally in Jerusalem or figuratively wherever he manifests his presence in the world—including within his people.

Paul picked up on this image and quoted verse 18 to describe Jesus' victory over the powers of darkness (Ephesians 4:8). Jesus stripped the enemy of power and distributed the spoils of war to his people, ascending to heaven in a military procession. Paul recognized this psalm as a prophecy of the invisible war that has been raging behind the scenes of creation in heavenly places. This victorious King is not power-hungry and selfish like others; he generously sets the lonely in families (Psalm 68:5-6) and shares his gifts with his people. We now live in the victory he has won.

RE-ENVISION YOUR PLACE IN THE KINGDOM

Perhaps you've seen yourself as a servant of God or even a friend of Jesus—both of which are true. But Scripture describes you as even more: a participant in his victory, a sharer of the spoils of war, a royal priest who is seated in heavenly places and reigns with him (1 Peter 2:9; Ephesians 2:6), and a bearer of authority over powers of darkness (Ephesians 6:12-13). Some Christians want to avoid appearing presumptuous or sounding like distorters of the gospel who emphasize these things to the exclusion of all else, yet Scripture casts a lofty vision for us. Step into it. In the same Spirit demonstrated by our conquering King—compassionate, humble, benevolent, yet authoritative—live out the thorough victory he has already given you.

PSALM 69: THE MESSIANIC VICTORY

The descendants of those who obey him will inherit the land, and those who love him will live there in safety.

69:36

Despite the victorious tone of the last four psalms, this one returns to the struggles of the king. It is referred to often in the New Testament as a portrayal of the messianic King. Jesus quoted verse 4 about being hated without cause (John 15:25). Hints of verse 36 appear in the third beatitude, describing those who will inherit the land or the earth (Matthew 5:5). John quoted verse 9 to point out Jesus' zeal for his Father's house (John 2:17). John alluded to verse 21 in reference to the sour wine offered to Jesus on the cross (John 19:28-30). Peter quoted verse 25 to describe the judgment of Judas (Acts 1:20). And Paul quoted verses 22-23 to describe Jews hardening their hearts toward the Messiah for a time (Romans 11:9-10). Clearly Jesus and the apostolic writers saw this psalm as a messianic prophecy.

That being the case, we are justified in looking through this lens and seeing beyond the context of ancient Israel and into the cosmic war. The imprisoned ones are human beings held captive by the results of the Fall (Psalm 69:33). The deliverance of God's people, the reestablishment of the land or the earth, and the assurances that his people will inherit it and live in it in safety (vv. 35-36) aptly describe our redemption and restoration. The psalm points toward intense trials that end in a thorough and final victory.

RE-ENVISION THE WORLD

The world belongs to those who love God. It may not look that way—you may feel like an alien in foreign territory (and for a time, you are)—but your Father already owns everything, and Jesus stands to inherit it all. Every believer is a fellow heir who gets to share in that inheritance.

When you feel besieged, see the world not as the besiegers' territory but as your Father's (and yours). As much as they act like they own the place, they don't. We hope they come around and believe in him, too, joining us as rightful heirs—but many will not. Either way, his Kingdom is coming, and his will is going to be done "*on earth* as it is in heaven" (Matthew 6:10, emphasis added). That's both our prayer and our destiny, certain to be fulfilled.

PSALM 70: A LONGER, GREATER RESCUE

Please, God, rescue me! Come quickly, LORD, and help me.

70:1

The Psalms are full of suffering. It comes in various forms—physical danger, emotional turmoil, betrayal and loss, anxiety about the future, and more—and in various contexts—sometimes in the midst of an intense, immediate crisis, other times in the course of a long season of pain. Reading the Psalms, we might get the impression that life is mostly about hardship punctuated at times with bursts of hope and worship. But this collection of songs and poems was not meant to represent a preponderance of life experiences; it was meant to guide us through them. And as people who encounter challenges from time to time, we need to know where to turn for help.

We also need encouragement to press in toward God and wait for his touch and his timing. Like the psalmist, we're prone to pray for his intervention to come "quickly," and from God's perspective, it does. In fact, he has already set up his intervention before we ever cry out. But his "quickly" and our "quickly" are not the same thing, and his help is not dictated by our sense of urgency. Sometimes there is more to gain in letting situations unfold. The victory is more comprehensive than a mere deliverance. The deeper the crisis gets, the more people it may affect, and his intervention becomes more thorough and more visible.

RE-ENVISION YOUR TIMETABLE

In your crises, are your prayers all about getting you out of trouble as soon as possible or maximizing the testimony and its ripple effects for the good of the Kingdom? If you simply see a need to escape whatever trouble you're in, his delays won't make sense. But if you envision a process of amplifying the victory and creating a more robust testimony, they will. Learn to look for his greater purposes, ask him what he's doing, and patiently let it unfold. Seeing the bigger picture gives you greater endurance and wins greater victories in the end.

PSALM 71: A HEART PREPARED TO RECEIVE

I will keep on hoping for your help;
I will praise you more and more.

71:14

With the perspective of a lifetime, the psalmist looks back at God's faithfulness. He has a long memory of the relationship (vv. 5-6, 17-18). He knows God has treated him well and that his life is a testimony to others (v. 7). Yet even now, in his later years, he is once again appealing to God to be rescued "from the clutches of cruel oppressors" (v. 4). It's a familiar cry, and he expects a familiar response.

In all his years, the psalmist has learned a valuable spiritual principle: Praise comes before the answer (as well as after). In fact, it comes before everything. He will keep on expecting God's help, but in the meantime, he will praise him more and more. Among the false religions surrounding Israel, people often made their worship contingent on an answer. But worshipers of Yahweh are called to fill their mouths with praise and gratitude all the time. We may have moments of desperation, but our lives are still to be glistening with expectancy.

RE-ENVISION DESPERATION

You might think you pray from a desperate position, but you never do. Even when you feel desperate, God has already bound you to Jesus in heavenly realms and given you multiple promises and assurances that he is working on your behalf. Will the answers always look like you expect them to? Probably not. And you may have to go through adversity on the way to them. But if he's always working all things for the good of those who love him (Romans 8:28), then praise always accurately honors what he is doing. Instead of seeing yourself as desperate, put on new lenses and see just how privileged you are. A heart full of gratitude is wonderfully prepared to believe and receive, enabling us to see his help more easily.

PSALM 72: A MUCH BETTER VIEW

Men shall be blessed in Him; all nations shall call Him blessed.

72:17, NKJV

If Book 2 has shifted the focus of the Psalms beyond Israel's borders in order to engage all nations, there's hardly a better way to conclude it than with this psalm. It's a royal, messianic psalm attributed to Solomon, and it calls for the whole earth to be filled with God's glory and to praise him for it. It exalts the king and his reign in the strongest terms.

Poems honoring ancient kings were normally filled with hyperbole, and this one fits that description. But what might be hyperbole for an earthly king applies to the messianic King rather accurately. His reign will outlast the sun and moon (v. 5); he will rule to the ends of the earth (v. 8); all kings will bow to him, and all nations will serve him (v. 11). Prophetic declarations about the messianic reign seem to use these sorts of descriptions quite literally. Even the Abrahamic covenant (Genesis 12:1-3) points to it (Psalm 72:17). This psalm of fulfillment ties these lofty themes together.

RE-ENVISION THE STATE OF THE WORLD

In an age of discouragement, many Christians assume such prophecies of "all nations" (v. 11, 17) and "the whole earth" (v. 19) are deferred until the return of Jesus, mere dreams to cling to until that time. And it's true that the fullness of his Kingdom will come then. But if we really saw what God was doing around the world today—not reported in the news, of course—we would be amazed. People are coming to Jesus in unexpected places and in unexpected ways; old institutions may be flagging, but new movements are gathering momentum; and God's Word is accessible in more places now than ever before. There's a reason the powers of darkness are raging so desperately. They clearly see what God's Spirit is doing, and they are fighting against it.

Lift up your eyes and live with immense optimism. Anticipate great blessings to come. Whether natural eyes see why or not, we have ample reason to "praise his glorious name forever!" (v. 19).

BOOK 3: PSALMS 73–89

In Book 3, the psalms turn more corporate and more focused on national crises. Previous psalms have called on the nations (even Israel's enemies) to recognize the God of the whole earth, their true King, and to worship him. Yet many of those enemies remained threatening, and God's people remained in danger. After centuries of corruption and idolatry among the kings and people of Israel and Judah, the prophetic warnings of disaster grew stronger.

BACKGROUND

These psalms reflect the devastation of Israel at the hands of Assyria (722 BC) and the catastrophic invasions of Babylon into Judah (597 and 586 BC), resulting in the destruction of Jerusalem and the Temple (vividly described in Psalm 79). They also reflect the apparent end of David's dynasty—a dynasty God had promised to make everlasting (2 Samuel 7).

Such crises raise all sorts of questions. Why were the enemies of God's people given the upper hand? Why would God let his dwelling place on earth be overrun by idolatrous nations? What happened to God's promises to set a king on David's throne forever? If the scepter was never to depart from Judah (Genesis 49:10), why had it departed? And, most devastating of all in its implications, was God done with Israel?

The psalmists wrestle with these questions in Book 3 (and beyond), yet most remain hopeful. After all, long before the sacking of Jerusalem and the Babylonian captivity, prophets had foretold Israel's restoration back to its Promised Land—a second exodus of sorts—and given reassurances that David's dynasty was not quite as finished as it seemed. This promised restoration occurred when Persia's King Cyrus overthrew Babylon (539 BC) and allowed Jewish exiles to return to Jerusalem if they wanted to.

Some of these psalms were surely written well before these national crises (though it's guesswork to attempt to date psalms that refer to no specific historical event). But these themes of crisis, like the prophetic voices that foretold them, had long been present, even if they had not yet reached their crescendo in Assyrian and Babylonian conquest. Still, in the midst of threatening circumstances, numerous calls emerge to praise God and declare his goodness.

One of the prominent themes of this section of Psalms is the history of the Temple and its centrality in Israel's worship. From the Tabernacle of Moses to the Tabernacle of David to the Temple of Solomon until its eventual destruction in the sixth century BC, the importance of God's dwelling place among his people is woven throughout these psalms. Along with the Davidic covenant, the Temple is an organizing theme of Israel's history, and threats to either struck at the heart of the kingdom.

The first eleven psalms in this book (73–83) are attributed to Asaph, who was appointed from among the Levites to be a leading musician when David brought the Ark to Jerusalem. His descendants, the "sons of Asaph," continued to lead Temple worship for centuries and were involved in the restoration in the time of Ezra and Nehemiah after the Exile. If these psalms were written by Asaph himself, then they were composed during the time of David. If "psalm of Asaph" can also mean "in the Asaph tradition" or "of the sons of Asaph," which is plausible, then they could have been written at any point in Israel's history after David's reign, including after the return from captivity.

Five psalms in this book are attributed to the descendants of Korah, who were introduced in Book 2. Two of these psalmists from the time of Solomon are named specifically—Heman (Psalm 88) and Ethan (Psalm 89)—though these could also be descendants of Temple musicians by these names. The last of these psalms, Psalm 89, which ends this book, captures well the overriding message of God's faithfulness throughout all generations. Regardless of the era in which these psalms were written, they were compiled in this book by an editor who wanted to focus on the themes of God's enduring promises in the midst of hardship, even if hardship rose to the level of a catastrophic collapse and existential crisis.

THE BIG PICTURE

There will be times in our lives when our vision of God's plan doesn't play out as expected—when all seems lost; when we wonder if we've missed his best, forfeited the opportunity he gave us, or even stepped outside of his will irrevocably, leaving us with nothing but some version of a divine consolation prize. Our minds may be flooded with questions, but our hearts need to remain focused on who he is and the certainty of what he has said. A God with perfect foreknowledge doesn't give promises that will be thwarted. He is always inviting us into his presence to receive his best for us, regardless of where we've been.

In any season of life, the approach of the psalmist in Psalm 84 can refocus our vision on the big picture. God's "dwelling place" (which, by the way, is now in his people) is lovely and a place of blessing (vv. 1, 4). Even the "Valley of Weeping" can be turned into a place of refreshment (v. 6). A day in God's courts is better than all our other experiences combined (v. 10). And our God is always our sun and shield who fills our lives with grace and glory (v. 11). These truths endure through any crisis, no matter how large or threatening. They are to captivate our hearts in all our highs and lows and twists and turns. Eyes set on these themes will not be distracted by lesser visions—and we will recognize that all other visions are indeed lesser than this.

PSALM 73: THE LENSES OF TRUTH

Whom have I in heaven but you? I desire you more than anything on earth. My health may fail, and my spirit may grow weak, but God remains the strength of my heart; he is mine forever.

73:25-26

Asaph (or one of his descendants) saw the prosperity of the wicked and felt like he was losing his faith over it. It didn't fit the promises of the covenant, as he understood it. After all, God had clearly said he would bless the faithful and discipline the ungodly. From Asaph's perspective, as he watched the corruption of his society and the success of his enemies, God seemed not to be keeping the terms of his own agreement.

The catalyst that changed Asaph's understanding was spending time in God's sanctuary (v. 17)—specifically the Temple or Tabernacle. An encounter with God's presence always changes the way we see things, and Asaph realized he was using present circumstances to make final judgments. Looking at the middle of the story, the wicked were indeed doing well; looking at the end of it, they were not. When God placed the lenses of truth over Asaph's eyes, Asaph saw how precarious the position of the ungodly actually is.

RE-ENVISION THE WHOLE PICTURE

We have a natural tendency to assume that the way things are now is the way they always will be. Spiritual eyes see a much bigger picture: the whole plot, ultimate endings, the destiny God has in store for those who love him and those who don't. And that changes everything.

Seeing what's at stake in our lives sends us into the presence and protection of God. Like the psalmist, we realize what lasts and want to anchor ourselves in him. There is nothing of greater value in heaven or on earth, nothing more desirable, no worthier affection. Whatever happens around us, whatever illusions the world presents to us, we end up with him, strong and secure forever.

PSALM 74: A DISORIENTING PROCESS

Remember your covenant promises, for the land is full of darkness and violence!

74:20

In 597 BC, the Babylonians invaded Judah, plundered the Temple in Jerusalem, and took many of the city's leaders into captivity. In 586 BC, they invaded the city again and destroyed it, including the Temple itself. This psalm seems to have been written in the aftermath of one of these invasions, and it reflects how shocking and disorienting the experience must have been. In light of God's unfathomable power in creating the forces of nature (vv. 12-17), he surely should have been able to handle the insults and attacks of aggressive nations (vv. 18-19). Yet Judah seemed to have been forsaken, and the psalmist was offended.

The people of Judah were struck by numerous contradictions to the promises God had given them. Miracles seemed to be a distant memory, nothing more than a historical anomaly, and there was little evidence that God's favor and blessing were still on them. Their vulnerability to a foreign power raised questions about the God who had said he would be their rock and refuge. For a kingdom that prided itself on God's presence in its Temple and believed David's dynasty would last forever—by God's own word—the corruption and destruction of that Temple and an interruption to that dynasty would have been catastrophic, an existential crisis of epic proportions.

RE-ENVISION PLAN A

The Babylonian invasions were God's response to centuries of Judah's corruption and idolatry, but there are plenty of situations other than discipline and judgment that defy our expectations—and perhaps provoke bitterness toward God. Maybe we felt sure of God's leading but turned out to be wrong. Maybe we misinterpreted a divine promise or how it applied to us. Or maybe we thought we understood his timing but didn't. When this happens, it rocks our world. Yet our world is still anchored on the Rock.

Go ahead and envision God's revealed purposes for your life, but hold the details loosely. He *will* remember his covenant promises and fulfill his plan for you. In one form or another, at one time or another, he will get you where he promised to take you.

PSALM 75: LIVING IN LIGHT OF THE END

God says, "I will break the strength of the wicked, but I will increase the power of the godly."

75:10

Most people are well-informed about the components of a healthy lifestyle, yet many of us still indulge in behaviors that could, in the long run, result in threatening conditions. Some get by better than others, but many come to regret their unwise decisions. Health issues have a way of reinforcing consequences we should have expected long ago.

The same is true for our ethical decisions and beliefs. Truth and morality might appear relative in a world where divine justice does not come instantly, or even soon. But just because the absolutes aren't readily apparent doesn't mean they aren't there. Decades of defying them without consequence doesn't mean consequences aren't coming. God will hold everyone accountable in the end.

The psalmist affirmed God's eventual judgment. While many in his society acted as if that judgment would never come, the psalmist knew better. The wicked persisted in their recklessness, but they would not get off unscathed; and the godly would not be trampled on forever. A reckoning would come, and God would set everything right.

RE-ENVISION TODAY

How would you live today if you knew you would face Jesus tomorrow? Whatever your answer is, learn to see that as your baseline. In reality, you're facing him right now; he is as present in the room as any friend or family member would be. But when we know and expect his assessment of our lives, it can help intensify our devotion and refocus us on our calling. We streamline our lives when we're pursuing a singular goal.

Envision his presence—not as a figment of your imagination but as the reality it is—and let it shape every moment of your day. Trust that he "will increase the power of the godly," and position yourself to receive his favor. Live with the expectation that he will make things right—for you, in you, and through you.

PSALM 76: PRESENCE AND POWER

There he has broken the fiery arrows of the enemy, the shields and swords and weapons of war.

76:3

Though Judah and Jerusalem had enemies and may have been under siege by them, the psalmist took comfort in God's presence in Jerusalem (vv. 1-2), his awesome power and majesty (vv. 4-9), and his sovereignty over the earth and its mortal kings (vv. 11-12). God even uses defiant human beings to enhance his own glory (v. 10). Nothing can defeat him.

Yet his chosen people often seemed defeated, which was hard to reconcile with his covenant promises. So the psalmist emphasized one of the core aspects of that covenant: God would honor his own name through his people. Because of his presence in Jerusalem and its Temple, and because God had long ago called his people into this land and pledged to love them irrevocably, he would continue to bring victory. Even in times of trouble, including those of their own making, they would still be able to depend on him.

God had defended Jerusalem many times before, and the psalmist connected his protection to his special presence at the Temple. "There he [broke] the fiery arrows of the enemy" and saved his people. The symbolism is revealing; those who experience his presence can rely on his supernatural protection.

RE-ENVISION YOUR STRENGTH

When you find yourself in a battle, your impulse will be to go on the attack. Sometimes God may lead you there, but he'll lead you somewhere else first: into his presence. That's where victories come from. Sometimes he wins them before you ever have to face the battlefield. But even if you become fully engaged in a spiritual conflict, he will build you up and arm you from a position of intimate fellowship. Your focus on him, not the enemy, is your source of strength.

Don't get distracted by the turmoil, threats, and obstacles around you. Let your vision be captivated by the God above them all. Fix your gaze on him and do not be moved. He is the warrior who fights for and rescues all who place their affections on him.

PSALM 77: POWER IN PRAISE

You are the God of great wonders! You demonstrate your awesome power among the nations.

77:14

The psalmist was in "deep trouble" (v. 2), "overwhelmed with longing" for God's help (v. 3), unable to sleep, and "too distressed even to pray" (v. 4). He remembered the "good old days" and the "joyful songs" that used to fill his nights (vv. 5-6), but now he wonders: Is God ignoring him? "Has he slammed the door on his compassion?" (v. 9). It's hard to discern anything but pessimism in the first half of this lament.

"But then I recall . . ." writes the psalmist (v. 11), and from there the focus is on all God has done in the past, as if the psalmist is insisting, "But I know who you are!" It's a choice to refocus and re-envision the truth, and it leads to something wonderful: the kind of faith that changes things.

Choosing to dwell on God's works builds faith and creates a climate for miracles. When we view him as the God who has rejected us, closed the door on his compassion, or withheld his favor for whatever reason—the view of the first ten verses—faith fails. But if we choose to remember, to see who he really is, faith rises. Sometimes we have to deny what our natural eyes are telling us in the moment in favor of what we know to be true. And that profoundly redirects the course of our lives.

RE-ENVISION HIS TRACK RECORD

This psalm is a model for praising God when we don't feel like it. Instead of focusing on what's wrong and asking him to fix it, we focus on how he has come through in the past—whether biblically and historically, in our own lives, in the life of someone we know, or *anywhere*—and we declare our confidence that he will do so again. Something shifts in our spirit when we fill our vision with his goodness, power, and love. As we've seen, he is enthroned on the praises of his people (Psalm 22:3). In faith, we praise him and see him, and our faith sets the stage for his great works to come.

PSALM 78: A KINGDOM FOR THE AGES

Each generation should set its hope anew on God, not forgetting his glorious miracles and obeying his commands.

78:7

This bird's-eye view of Israel's history from Moses to David emphasizes a cycle of falling away and then returning to the Lord, much like the more compressed cycle we see in the book of Judges. The previous psalm urged remembering God's past works. This one does that with a particular focus on how God's works relate to his people's devotion. Not surprisingly, he mercifully led them (in spite of their rebelliousness), offered his forgiveness, and strongly supported them when their hearts returned to him.

New Testament figures picked up on the prophetic images in this psalm, placing Jesus' ministry in the context of Israel's long history. The reference to learning from parables and "hidden lessons" in verse 2 points to Jesus' parables (as quoted in Matthew 13:35), and Jesus applied the image of "bread from heaven" in verse 24 to himself (John 6:30-35)—the ultimate mercy of God among a rebellious people.

The psalmist's primary goal in this psalm was to urge God's people to teach his ways and his works to each new generation so they would not repeat the sins of their ancestors (Psalm 78:1-8). In spite of all the wonderful things God had done, his people repeatedly rebelled and fell away. The psalmist knew this cycle would continue—unless each generation "set its hope anew on God" (v. 7) and was stirred to greater faithfulness.

RE-ENVISION HERITAGE

Constructing medieval cathedrals was a notoriously slow process. Many of the builders began their work where the last generation left off and set it up for the next generation to expand on, knowing they would never see the finished product. The Kingdom of God is like that; you're involved in a project that has developed over millennia, and now you are responsible for making progress and passing it on. Inheritance is a huge deal in God's Kingdom. Make sure your vision is bigger than your own life and pray that it outlasts you. You aren't just pursuing a calling. You're investing in generations to come.

PSALM 79: THE ULTIMATE PURPOSE

Help us, O God of our salvation! Help us for the glory of your name.

79:9

The Babylonians invaded and destroyed Jerusalem and its Temple in 586 BC, and this psalm describes the horrific aftermath. The psalmist expresses the agony of the people in trying to understand why God allowed this tragic event. In addition to the physical devastation, their identity as God's people was rocked. They were told that the scepter would not depart from Judah (Genesis 49:10), yet the scepter had departed. What were they to make of God's covenant promises and everything that had been prophesied about the future? If they looked closely enough, they would see promises of restoration in the prophecies of Isaiah, Jeremiah, and Ezekiel. Still, they had been led to believe there would be an unbroken line in David's dynasty (2 Samuel 7:16), and now the line had been broken.

Was God not concerned for his own reputation? Of course he was; numerous biblical passages tell us that his works glorify his name. But contrary to the beliefs of many in Jerusalem, God's people were not invincible simply because they bore God's name and hosted his presence in the Temple. If they tarnished his name through corruption and idolatry, he would discipline them. He upholds his people for their sake and his (see Ezekiel 20:14), but not when upholding them affirms their rebellion.

Still, the psalmist understood the fundamental purpose of creation—to glorify God. He made no appeal for God to help them out of obligation or because they deserved rescue. He recognized God as the center of the universe and aligned his prayer with reality.

RE-ENVISION YOUR PLACE IN THE UNIVERSE

Imagine the sun orbiting around a tiny planet rather than the planet orbiting the sun. It's an absurd picture, isn't it? Yet sometimes that's how we behave. God has given us so many assurances of his love and care that we can easily begin to act as if he's there to serve us—to orbit around our needs. The universe was designed by him and for him, and we experience alignment, divine favor, and spiritual momentum when we live in sync with his ultimate purposes. When we commit to what's on his heart, he eagerly shapes and fulfills what's on ours.

PSALM 80: THE WARRIOR SHEPHERD

Make your face shine down upon us. Only then will we be saved.

80:3

The previous psalm ended with a reference to God's people as the sheep of his pasture. This one begins with an appeal to the Shepherd who cares for them. But this is no ordinary shepherd. He is "enthroned above the cherubim," radiant in glory (v. 1), and he is the God of Heaven's Armies (vv. 4, 7, 14, 19). In the midst of a crisis—possibly the fall of the northern kingdom of Israel at the hands of the Assyrians—the psalmist pleads for this all-powerful Warrior-Shepherd to come rescue his sheep.

The psalmist has accused the Shepherd of feeding his sheep "the bread of tears" (v. 5, NIV). Ravenous wolves, the enemies of God's people, have circled and devoured. The psalmist surely understands the cause—the sheep's stubborn departure from the Shepherd's care—yet he cries for the Shepherd to come after them and rescue them. Is the Shepherd angry with them? Perhaps, but he is still the Shepherd, and they need his face to "shine down" on them once again.

RE-ENVISION YOUR PURSUIT

It's human nature to seek the "shine" rather than the source of light, but God repeatedly calls us to the Source: himself. We tend to want the deliverance from our troubles more than we want the Deliverer, the healing more than the Healer, the provision more than the Provider. When that's our motivation, we are envisioning a life in need of support, not a life flowing from the Source. They aren't the same thing. All too often, we use God for our own satisfaction rather than offering ourselves for his.

Nothing on your to-do list today is more important than seeking his face, whether you're in a crisis or not. Ask the Warrior-Shepherd what's on his heart. Make his desires your own. Fill your heart with his radiant glory, and the rest of your life will begin to shine.

PSALM 81: WHAT GOD WOULD DO

Oh, that my people would listen to me! Oh, that Israel would follow me, walking in my paths! How quickly I would then subdue their enemies! How soon my hands would be upon their foes!

81:13-14

In this psalm's call to repentance, God himself pleads with his people simply to listen to what he says (vv. 6-16)—a reasonable request many seem to have neglected. Those who strayed were given over to the consequences of their "stubborn desires" (v. 12), not to end the relationship but to prompt them (eventually) to see the futility of running their own lives. They had no idea what they were missing; God would have fed them with the finest wheat and honey (v. 16).

Even though the context is a call to repentance, the underlying message is that God *wants* to do great things for his people. That's his default position. He longs to bless us, shower us with his goodness, and lift us up in every area of life. We may still struggle or go through hard times not of our own making—these may be opportunities to demonstrate our faithfulness to him, in fact—but within the bigger picture, these seasons, though painful in the moment, will not last forever. God's heart is inclined toward those who love him, and he wants to show us how much.

RE-ENVISION HIS FAVOR

No matter how much we are told about God's goodness, some of us envision having to twist his arm to get what we need. Perhaps such a picture comes from past disappointments or prayers that weren't (or have not yet been) answered, but it also reflects a tendency to focus on what God has not done rather than on what he has. Scripture repeatedly gives us a different picture. God longs to show his goodness to all whose hearts are ready to receive it. When we pour ourselves out for him, he pours himself into us, and our lives demonstrate the wisdom and beauty of walking in his paths.

PSALM 82: WHEREVER THE KINGDOM ISN'T

Give justice to the poor and the orphan; uphold the rights of the oppressed and the destitute. Rescue the poor and helpless.

82:3-4

This psalm's diatribe against "heavenly beings" (v. 1) reveals the stark contrast between God's justice and the world's. The psalmist refers to the "gods" (v. 6) who oppress the downtrodden with their wicked judgments. Whether these "gods" are indeed heavenly beings or mere human rulers or judges given a divine standing—Jesus implied they were people in John 10:34—is hardly the point. On the one hand, we see God's desire to care for the poor, the widows and orphans, and the oppressed and marginalized. On the other, we see exploitation and abuse. A society that tolerates the latter is at odds with its Creator, and it's up to God's people to sort it out.

The responsibility for sorting it out was clear in ancient Israel, ostensibly a theocracy with a God-anointed king. In that context, political rulers could point to divine mandates without pushback. Not so in today's world. Yet in God's eyes, the well-being of society is about more than just politics. He still has a heart for the hurting. If his people want to be in sync with him, we must too.

RE-ENVISION YOUR RESPONSIBILITY

This is not a political issue for Christians. It's a Kingdom of God issue. And we can be sure that wherever we see poverty, oppression, exploitation, injustice, and any other form of social ill, we are seeing antitheses of the Kingdom. The Kingdom and its people bring fullness, joy, hope, healing, and restoration—the whole package of God's shalom—and any absence of shalom in our world is an invitation to do something about it. Learn to see the world in those terms. Look for the evidence or absence of the Kingdom, and turn your heart, prayers, words, and actions in the direction of advancing it. This is how God demonstrates his nature through his people and one of the ways his Kingdom comes "on earth as it is in heaven" (Matthew 6:10).

PSALM 83: BATTLES BEHIND THE SCENES

They devise crafty schemes against your people; they conspire against your precious ones.

83:3

The psalmist saw God's Kingdom and its enemies in very earthly terms. He named many of Israel's local enemies, whom he also saw as God's enemies, and pleaded with God not to remain silent in the face of their threats and schemes against God's "precious ones." In the psalmist's mind, God's entire agenda was at stake. The chosen people were under siege.

In the New Testament, Kingdom conflict takes on cosmic implications. Jesus gave his followers authority over "snakes" and "scorpions" and "all the power of the enemy," promising that nothing in their spiritual battle would hurt them (Luke 10:19). Paul reminded his readers that we are not ignorant of the enemy's schemes (2 Corinthians 2:11), we have mighty weapons not of this world (2 Corinthians 10:3-4), and we are to stand firm and arm ourselves with the spiritual armor of God in our fight against evil spirits in heavenly places (Ephesians 6:11-18). These and many other biblical passages prepare us for a supernatural conflict that rages behind the scenes of our lives. And in the spirit of this psalm, we can call upon God to rise up against our enemies and thwart them.

RE-ENVISION YOUR WARFARE

Many Christians live with a "siege" mentality. Although some Christians are hardly aware of any spiritual battles in their lives—they see their hardships simply as struggles to manage in daily life—others are hardly aware of anything else. They see every hardship as an enemy attack against their identity and calling. They may know they are citizens of heaven, but they are very focused on hell.

God wants us to be aware of the powers of darkness but never become fixated on them. They aren't worth the energy. Instead, focus your attention on living in the light. Yes, a cosmic war is raging, and the stakes are high. But anxiety and dread are impotent weapons. An upward gaze filled with worship and praise brings heaven's power down and unravels our enemy's schemes.

PSALM 84: LONGING FOR GOD

A single day in your courts is better than a thousand anywhere else!

84:10

This well-known psalm is an ode to God's dwelling place—the Tabernacle or Temple—and even more to the God who dwells there. The psalmist longs for "the courts of the LORD" (v. 2)—the inner court, where priests ministered, and the outer courts, where the congregation gathered to worship. There is no hint of religious obligation here. He wants to shout joyfully to God with his entire being.

The psalm emphasizes the privileges and blessings of being in the Lord's house (vv. 1-4), of journeying to it (vv. 5-8), and of knowing and trusting the Lord who dwells there (vv. 9-11).* It promises that God will withhold no good thing from those who walk uprightly with him (v. 11, ESV). It's also a celebration of Jerusalem (and therefore a psalm of Zion), of pilgrimage, and most significantly, of a relationship with the one true God. For faithful Israelites, living among surrounding nations beholden to entire pantheons of impetuous, unpredictable gods, this relationship had to have seemed like a miraculous honor. The physical place of God's presence was available to a privileged few. And one day in his house was better than a thousand elsewhere.

* C. Hassell Bullock, *Psalms: Vol. 2: Psalms 73–150*, TTCS (Grand Rapids, MI: Baker Books, 2017), 93.

RE-ENVISION YOUR PRESENCE

Availability is no longer an issue. We can spend a thousand days in his courts—and more—all because of Jesus' sacrifice for us. The veil of the Temple has been torn (Matthew 27:51); we've been invited to come boldly to the throne (Hebrews 4:16); and even more astonishingly, God has cleansed us and made us into his temple, his dwelling place on earth (1 Corinthians 6:19). When we envision dwelling in God's courts, we don't have to think of going somewhere or creating some special circumstance. We're there now. The goal is not to arrive but to be acutely aware of where we already are, bask in God's presence, and live sacred lives empowered by that intimate fellowship. Cultivate that vision, worship in that place, and let your longing for him be satisfied.

PSALM 85: THE KINGDOM NOW

I listen carefully to what God the LORD is saying, for he speaks peace to his faithful people.

85:8

Book 3 of Psalms has been filled with images of conflict and the devastation of Assyrian and Babylonian invasions. Yet the previous psalm spoke of the blessedness of being in God's courts, and this one speaks of the beauty of his reign among his people. Regardless of what is going on in the world, nothing can disrupt the fellowship God's people have with him or thwart his purposes. Even in a world of turmoil, he establishes seasons and places of peace.

As we've already seen in previous psalms, the Hebrew term *shalom,* often translated "peace," incorporates so much more than simply the absence of conflict. It implies fullness, wholeness, abundance, well-being, health, satisfaction, and completeness—a full expression of what God desires for his people. In fact, this is what his Kingdom is all about. Wherever his Kingdom is, there's shalom. Wherever his Kingdom isn't, shalom is hard to find.

That's why the depiction of God's reign in verses 9-13 is filled with images of extravagant blessing. To some, it's a picture of the Kingdom one day in the distant future, when Jesus comes and fully establishes his rule. Yet there's no reason to defer all its blessings until then. Our land *can* be filled with glory (v. 9). Righteousness and peace *can* "kiss" wherever heaven and earth meet (v. 10). Truth *does* spring up from the earth wherever his people let it (v. 11). His Kingdom is not just "one day" but is ever-increasing now.

RE-ENVISION PEACE

When we pray "may your Kingdom come soon" and "may your will be done on earth, as it is in heaven" (Matthew 6:10), what are we really asking? Certainly we want God's presence and power in our lives, as the previous psalm so beautifully expressed. But we also desire his shalom, the fullness of all he offers his people. The psalmist listened carefully to God because he knew God would speak shalom to his faithful ones. When you pray, envision shalom as the answer. See the goodness, wholeness, and peace of God invading this world—and see yourself as part of the invasion.

PSALM 86: A COMPREHENSIVE RELATIONSHIP

Teach me your ways, O LORD, that I may live according to your truth! Grant me purity of heart, so that I may honor you.

86:11

This psalm of David (by him, for him, or about him) is thorough. It's an unapologetic prayer for the Lord to give the psalmist happiness and joy (v. 4). It's an assurance that God is "so good, so ready to forgive," that we can always count on his unfailing love (v. 5). It's a declaration that no false god compares to the God of Israel (v. 8). It's a request to learn God's ways and have a pure (literally, "singular," "unified," or "undivided") heart in order to honor him (v. 11). And it's a prayer for God to demonstrate his favor in front of the psalmist's enemies (v. 17). In all its facets, this psalm assumes God's comprehensive goodness in everything.

RE-ENVISION YOUR COMPLETENESS

Many Christians see their lives in compartments: spiritual, physical, mental, relational, financial, professional, and so on. They have no doubt God is concerned with the spiritual aspect of their lives, as well as other related areas. But there is nothing in the Psalms or the rest of Scripture that confines God's interests to our spiritual well-being and disregards the "non-spiritual"—as if there were such a thing. Yet some Christians have trouble praying confidently about their work, finances, and certain relationships—especially those they don't know if God endorses. In other words, in some areas of life they keep a safe distance from him, not realizing that any distance is unsafe.

Paul prayed that his readers would be "filled with all the fullness of God" (Ephesians 3:19, ESV). That's why a singular, unified, purposeful heart is so vital. In this relationship, we give all of ourselves to God, and he gives all of himself to us. Anything less is a fragmented, frustrating existence. Every area of our lives fits into God's Kingdom, and his Kingdom shapes everything about us. He emphatically calls us to an integrated life, a comprehensive salvation, a relationship that saturates every atom of our beings.

PSALM 87: WHEN EVERY KNEE BOWS

I will count Egypt and Babylon among those who know me—also Philistia and Tyre, and even distant Ethiopia. They have all become citizens of Jerusalem! . . . And the Most High will personally bless this city.

87:4-5

These verses make an astonishing statement. Amid a collection of worship songs and poems that so often cast oppressive, aggressive nations as the enemies of God himself, this psalm contains the startling prophecy that several of Israel's worst historical nemeses will one day be citizens of Jerusalem—the place of God's presence among his people. Either it's a brash declaration that Israel would take over the world or a bold declaration that God's Kingdom (symbolized by the city) will eventually melt the hostility of the nations and bring them into the fold. The latter is far more likely—the psalmist seems to envision God's global mission—yet is still surprising in the Psalter, especially Book 3.

But there are hints of a salvation that reaches far beyond Israel in God's covenant with Abraham (for example, Genesis 12:1-3), in the Prophets (for example, Isaiah 49:6; 60:3), and even in other psalms (as in 22:27; 98:2-4). By the time we get to Revelation, we see the enormity of God's plan. Vast multitudes from every tribe and tongue gather around the throne (Revelation 7:9-10, NKJV), and a brilliant new Jerusalem descends from heaven as the center of God's rule over an entirely restored creation (Revelation 21:1-2). Many from even the most hardened, rebellious nations will bow before the world's true King.

RE-ENVISION YOUR EXPECTATIONS

If you've bought into the scenario of hostile nations being cast away from God's presence at the return of the King, catch a new vision of what God is doing. Yes, there will be people from all nations who do not know him (though they, too, will have to acknowledge him), but there will also be many from all nations who stunningly, dramatically turn to him. Make no assumptions about the direction of people groups today; *now* is not a statement on *forever*. Instead, pray for, contribute to, participate in, and expect a global "great awakening." As Revelation 11:15 assures us, the kingdoms of this world will, without question, become the Kingdom of our Lord.

PSALM 88: HONEST TO GOD

O LORD, I cry out to you. I will keep on pleading day by day.

88:13

It's hard to find anything encouraging in this psalmist's dismal words. Like Job, he questions God's dealings with him, laments his illnesses and proximity to death, grieves his lost friendships, assumes God's anger toward him, and offers up only his tears. He has lived a hard life—sick since his youth (v. 15)—and has come to see God as the source of terrors (v. 16). The celebration of God's goodness in the previous four psalms is completely absent here.

We know this is not an accurate picture of God. As Scripture attests throughout, he is the source of life and light, the delight of his faithful ones, the Father who longs to bless his children, the Shepherd who takes care of his sheep. Yet in our limited experience, and in certain seasons, his hand seems hard and heavy. Explanations fall short. We have to live with some mystery and believe—against all immediate evidence at times—that what we see with natural eyes in the moment does not define who he is.

RE-ENVISION YOUR TRANSPARENCY

In the meantime, God welcomes our transparency. We don't have to clean up our thoughts and reject our impulses to tell him how we feel. He is fine with the kind of raw, desperate conversation the psalmists engage in. You can be completely honest about whatever is on your heart. But he doesn't want you to dwell on the crisis and become absorbed in self-pity, which will only magnify your problems and make you lose your focus on the bigger picture. Neither does he want to leave you in the depths. He wants you to bring everything to him, even in excruciating detail. From that place of authenticity, you bond with him, and he begins to transform you. He lifts the eyes of his people to see him more clearly. And to those who remain patient, he demonstrates his goodness in time.

PSALM 89: IN THE LIGHT OF HIS PRESENCE

Happy are those who hear the joyful call to worship, for they will walk in the light of your presence, LORD.

89:15

Book 3 ends with an epic psalm, in the sense that it recounts the history of God's covenant with Israel through David and then paints a picture of existential crisis: a battle for survival in which that everlasting covenant seems to have been lost forever. As we know, the prophecy would be fulfilled in Jesus, in ways far beyond what the psalmist could have imagined. The overarching theme of Book 3 (Psalms 73–89) has been devastation, whether at the hands of Assyria, Babylon, or some other enemy. Yet these periods of destruction and captivity have been punctuated with sweet moments of delight in God and praise for his faithfulness. Even against a backdrop of suffering, his people know that he and his purposes are good.

So the psalmist begins with praise—sweeping declarations about God's faithfulness—even though his biggest question is whether God has broken his oath to David. Rather than seeing God through the lens of the problem, he looks at the problem through the lens of God.

RE-ENVISION THE JOURNEY

When all seems lost—and even when it doesn't—there is no greater calling than to worship God and walk in the light of his presence. We might seek explanations, direction, and certain outcomes, and he often gives them to us. But he is much more interested in our personal journey—the process itself and how our relationship with him unfolds throughout. When we lock our hearts onto a particular outcome, we often panic when God's plan doesn't seem to fit. But hearts full of worship can handle unanswered questions and distant promises far better. They are also much more fulfilled, because they have learned to simply bask in his presence.

Most of the time, we can take our focus off the future and fix it on our right-now moments with God. Enjoy him now, sit in his presence, and just be with him. He'll get you where you need to go, but you're far more likely to get there with your eyes on him rather than on wherever "there" happens to be. The epic trajectory of your life is defined not by a problem or even a purpose but by a Person.

BOOK 4: PSALMS 90–106

The battle for hope in Book 3 was intense. In Babylon, the exiles were seen by their captors as a marginal, defeated people with a defeated God. Their hearts cried out—not only for freedom and restoration but also for vindication, themes clearly evident throughout Psalms. Book 4 reflects a greater ability to see the big picture: how the Babylonian captivity was part of Israel's story rather than the end of it.

As the psalmists begin to look beyond the Exile and the apparent interruption of David's line, hope for restoration arises. In the long and arduous process of Judah's captivity and return to the Promised Land, their understanding of the Kingdom of God has grown. In some ways, it is seen less as the reconstruction of David and Solomon's kingdom and more as the promise of a broader messianic Kingdom. This larger Kingdom of God incorporates both earthly and heavenly dimensions and people beyond Israel. Yes, the hope for Davidic kings remains. But even more, an assurance that Yahweh is King forever solidifies.

BACKGROUND

Many of the psalms in Book 4 were likely written in earlier centuries, but the editors or compilers who arranged them in this collection lived in this post-exilic time of restoration. Cyrus the Great of Persia overthrew Babylon in 539 BC and soon after issued a decree that Babylon's Jewish captives could return to Jerusalem to rebuild the Temple (2 Chronicles 36:22-23; Ezra 1:1-4). Some did return, though many remained where they were, scattered throughout Persian lands—part of the Jewish Diaspora. Wherever they were, they could look hopefully toward Jerusalem again—and, once it was rebuilt, the Temple where God dwelt among his people.

Israel's faith could have been destroyed by the Captivity and the end of David's dynasty. Instead, psalmists (and the editors who organized older psalms) recast the people's hopes on the deeper, longer trajectory of God's promises, cultivating expectations for a future messianic King and a restored kingdom.

Book 4 contains all the ups and downs of human experience, as the rest of the psalms do, but it also emphatically celebrates God's protection, provision, and perpetual faithfulness. After two psalms that promise blessing and protection for God's people (Psalms 90–91), Psalms 92–100 repeatedly declare that Yahweh is King. Three psalms reiterate the importance of David's kingship (Psalms 101–103)—a bold statement of faith in light of the interruption to his dynasty. And fittingly, the first biblical occurrences of *hallelujah* occur toward the end of this collection (Psalms 104–106; see "Hallelujah Psalms" on page 238). The last psalm in this book recounts the first Exodus and encourages exiles to respond well to God in this second exodus (from exile). God is renewing his Kingdom. Yes, questions remain, and specifics regarding the future seem very uncertain. But the future itself is nevertheless in his hands.

THE BIG PICTURE

The psalms of Book 4 present a picture of mature faith.* Tried and tested faith is able to endure through contradictions and equips us to see the bigger picture, even after everything we thought we knew has been thrown into question. If

* Robertson, *Flow of the Psalms*, 147–149.

young, zealous faith overflows with assurance of what God is doing and eagerly commits to be a part of it, mature faith accepts that we don't always understand God's plan but still reaffirms our commitment to him. Mature faith doesn't deny the overall trajectory of God's purposes, but it also recognizes that the path to his purposes isn't always the one we expect. Even so, it clings to his goodness and chooses to praise him for all he has done, is doing, and will do in the future.

Psalm 103, one of the best loved in the Psalter, captures that perspective well. It prioritizes praise and casts God's forgiveness, healing, redemption, abundance, and restoration against a backdrop of sin, disease, lack, and death, all of which pale in comparison to his goodness. This psalm declares that his love and mercy extend far beyond his anger and punishment (v. 10-11). He is like a father to his children—and his children's children (v. 13, 17-18). He rules everywhere and always and is worthy of wholehearted praise from human and angelic beings (v. 19-22).

A seasoned faith clings to that vision. God's comfort is always greater than our pain, his healing always more potent than our diseases, his forgiveness always greater than our sin, and his life always overcoming whatever looks like death. As Paul assured his readers, our journey with God may come with heavy costs, but the "weight of glory" awaiting us far exceeds them all (Romans 8:18; 2 Corinthians 4:17, ESV). In his Kingdom, even now, the benefits are always worth the cost.

Like the psalmist, choose to fill your gaze with the benefits of life with God (Psalm 103:2-6). Orient your attitudes, words, and actions around his blessings. And always choose to see your challenges as molehills and his goodness as the overwhelming mountain it is.

PSALM 90: THE NUMBERING OF DAYS

Teach us to realize the brevity of life, so that we may grow in wisdom.

90:12

The compiler of Book 4 of the Psalms likely saw Israel's history from a place of exile, after Jerusalem and its Temple were destroyed and the Davidic dynasty ended. It makes sense, then, that he would begin this collection with a psalm that stretches all the way back to Moses—when the people of Israel had been captive in Egypt and were delivered by God's miraculous power. Some of the verbiage of this psalm echoes the Song of Moses in Deuteronomy 32 and the words of Moses' intercession in Exodus 32. Unlike many of the psalms in the previous three books that were so focused on struggle, establishing the kingdom, and understanding devastation at the hands of enemies, this psalm emphasizes restoration, even anticipating that God would replace all the evil years with good (v. 15). The voice of Moses, reaching across the centuries, reminded the Israelites that God (not Jerusalem) was their dwelling place through all generations, even if some of those generations seemed fleeting.

RE-ENVISION YOUR TIME

On the one hand, our lives are short, and we need to use our time wisely. On the other hand, God is our dwelling place, and abiding in the Eternal One gives us a timeless nature. This truth is expressed from multiple directions in the New

Testament as Christ in us, us in Christ, and the Holy Spirit dwelling within us. We live with an eternal perspective, realizing that we have a brief window in time to leverage our actions for eternal fruitfulness.

That requires a conceptual shift, a re-envisioning of our days. We already have eternal life—beginning now, not just later—but our temporal lifespans on the present earth create a unique opportunity. All of life is an occasion to plant seeds in everlasting soil for an eternal harvest. Our fleeting resources (time, talents, gifts, money, and relational connections) must not be wasted. Envision this opportunity daily and make the most of it. It's an investment with returns that never stop coming in.

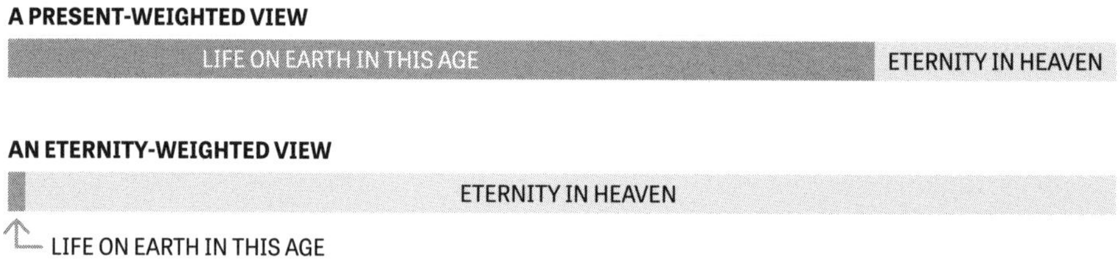

A PRESENT-WEIGHTED VIEW

LIFE ON EARTH IN THIS AGE | ETERNITY IN HEAVEN

AN ETERNITY-WEIGHTED VIEW

ETERNITY IN HEAVEN

LIFE ON EARTH IN THIS AGE

A weighted perspective: With a present-weighted view of life, we focus most of our thoughts and energy on our here-and-now experiences, perhaps valuing eternity but not orienting everything in our lives around it. With an eternity-weighted view, we still value life in the here and now and plan accordingly, but we consider everything in light of eternal experience and fruitfulness. This shapes all our hopes, fears, desires, plans, relationships, and much more.

He will order his angels to protect you wherever you go. They will hold you up with their hands so you won't even hurt your foot on a stone.

91:11-12

Satan quoted this psalm (Matthew 4:6). He wanted to test Jesus with it, to get him to exploit it as a demonstration of God's special care for his Son. Of course, the psalm applies to anyone who trusts God. It promises that those who love him will be rewarded with a long, flourishing life full of his blessings (Psalm 91:14-16).

It's a comforting promise—but not an absolute one, as exemplified by numerous prophets, apostles, and other martyrs. Yet these words reassure us that this is God's heart and his will toward his people and very often the testimony he gives them. Faithful people in dangerous situations have relied on the promises of this psalm and been miraculously protected and delivered.

As with any of God's promises, attaching faith to them is vital. His Spirit brings these assurances to mind in situations of need, and we can trust them implicitly. Those who have made God their dwelling place can be certain, even in a world of danger and uncertainty, that God is actively watching over them.

RE-ENVISION YOUR PROTECTOR

Some Christians, acutely aware of the threats around them, strive for safety. They live very conservatively, even in fear, avoiding risks in hope of living as long as possible. Others feel led to venture into treacherous situations with nothing but these promises to count on and a belief that the safest place to be is in God's will—wherever that is. What's the difference? The latter group has a strong vision of God as their bodyguard.

Envision all of heaven's resources—the power of the Holy Spirit, angelic warriors, a great cloud of witnesses—ready to act on your behalf. God guarantees no specific lifespan, of course, and we can't assume that the faithful won't die young. But we can be sure they won't die by accident, as if God had abandoned his post or left them to their own devices. He is "watching to see that [his] word is fulfilled" (Jeremiah 1:12, NIV), and his Word presents him as your protector and peace.

PSALM 92: A SABBATH FOREVER

The godly will flourish like palm trees and grow strong like the cedars of Lebanon. For they are transplanted to the LORD's own house. They flourish in the courts of our God.

92:12-13

Psalm 1 pictured the righteous as a fruitful tree drawing nourishment from a river. Psalm 52 pictured the godly as a deeply rooted olive tree that would keep growing no matter how far it was cut back. Here the godly "flourish like palm trees and grow strong like the cedars." They are tall and secure, lush and fruitful, remaining green even in old age (v. 14). Simply being around God fills them with life.

This psalm is a song for the Sabbath, and as such it is full of praise. It voices no needs, includes no requests. It simply declares God's goodness, as well as the goodness—the beauty and appropriateness—of worshiping him. There is no hint of discouragement or defeat in this psalm, no threats from enemies or laments about injustice. It offers an image of the environment of praise—and how life thrives there.

RE-ENVISION YOUR ENVIRONMENT

Envision God's courts as something like a greenhouse under the sun of his glory. No matter how desolate and bitter the environment outside, inside it's full of warmth and nourishment and life. This is where we connect with the source of life and receive everything we need to grow. It's an eternal Sabbath of praise. The wicked may flourish for a moment (v. 7), but the flourishing of worshipers lasts forever.

This is the Kingdom environment, and we are called to saturate ourselves in its vitality and advance it into the surrounding world. Like Eden in Genesis 1:28, the greenhouse is meant to grow us. Our flourishing is not just for our own benefit but also for the benefit of others. Through God's Spirit overflowing from his people, everyone we encounter should sense life in our presence and begin to flourish as well, all to the honor and glory of God.

ROYAL PSALMS

David was the king of Israel. So were his successors. And so was God. Themes of royalty and reigning permeate the Psalms, even many that do not explicitly mention a king. Some refer to a coronation or an enthronement, some ask for a blessing on the king, and some simply envision a well-governed society under a godly ruler. Royal psalms are also referred to as "kingship psalms" or "psalms of enthronement," each term bearing somewhat different meanings. A list of royal psalms might include Psalms 2, 20–21, 28, 45, 47, 72, 93, 95–99, 101, 110, 132, and 144, but lists vary widely. It's a difficult category to define, yet kingship runs unmistakably throughout the Psalter. And it's not an obsolete topic to us. Royal psalms still speak profoundly to believers like us, who serve *the* King.

Much debate has surrounded the form, function, and content of these psalms—how they were used in Israel's worship, what they tell us about the nation's understanding of kingship, even whether some of them are actually referring to kings. But at minimum we can say that the themes of human and divine kingship provide a strong background to many psalms, and those themes often assume that God's chosen and anointed kings would collectively fulfill his promises to David of an everlasting dynasty. Some of these psalms are by or about David specifically, some about his successors over the following centuries, and some about "the anointed" in general—in most cases, presenting a messianic vision.

It's not always clear whether certain psalms are spoken in the voice of the king or a non-royal psalmist, but the distinction doesn't necessarily change how we understand them. Clearly, ancient Israel (like many other societies) understood that what was good for the king was good for the people, and vice versa. They may not have been in the same situation as the king, but they had the same enemies, turmoil, hopes, joys, and faith. God's dealings with one would apply to the other. A blessing on the king was a blessing on everyone under him. Even a promise to the king could apply equally to those loyal to him.

What this means is that wherever the psalms encourage David or a later king in a time of distress, we can apply it to our distresses too. Whatever these psalms promise David or the future Messiah, we can embrace it, too, as heirs of the Kingdom. Their lives and ours are connected. Our future is a continuation of their history. As a royal priesthood granted that status by the Messiah's victory (1 Peter 2:9; Revelation 1:6), we are still invited to envision the character, the blessings, and the mission of the Kingdom as our own.

Your royal laws cannot be changed. Your reign, O Lord, is holy forever and ever.

93:5

At whatever point in Israel's history this psalm was written—some suggest during the Exile—it originated in a world full of threats and uncertainty. God's people didn't always know how to make sense of it all, but they knew their rock-bottom truth: God was still on his throne. Over all creation's forces, over all enemies, over all other gods, he reigned supreme.

That's still true, of course. We're reminded constantly of all kinds of threats—nuclear, technological, economic, environmental, even extraterrestrial—many of which are deemed existential. A steady stream of headlines and caustic debate fills us with toxic anxiety and dread. Yet the Lord is "robed in majesty and armed with strength" (v. 1), his decrees are certain to come about, and his house is holy forever (v. 5). In a very insecure world, some things are still absolute.

In our modern context, on this side of the Cross, we might understand these same basic truths of the psalm in different words: Our Father is the biggest Dad in the universe, the father every kid in the neighborhood would want to have, if they only knew. Whatever he says is completely trustworthy, so his promises to us are unbreakable. And his house—which, in our day, means the people in whom his Spirit dwells—is holy, set apart for his purposes, a treasured possession for a special use. Whatever else is going on in our lives and in our world, this is the big picture.

RE-ENVISION YOUR STORYLINE

One of the greatest spiritual challenges we face is to continue living in the big picture. Our lives are full of small details, and we often get caught up in the minor storylines (and think they're major). But when we catch a glimpse of God on his throne, everything else pales in comparison. When we consciously live in the larger story, the details of the smaller story don't seem to matter as much. Fear fades, our sense of security swells, and we dream again of great things God wants to do through us. We are little children with a big Dad, and we can trust his promise that he never leaves his throne.

Joyful are those you discipline, LORD, those you teach with your instructions.

94:12

The people of Israel and Judah had seen some bad things, and the psalmist itemizes some of the actions and attitudes of the worst offenders. The wicked, the proud, the corrupt—all those responsible for society's problems and perhaps God's judgments against the land—thought God didn't hear or see (or exist). They assumed they were getting away with whatever they wanted to do—quite a shortsighted view. Like many people, the wrongdoers did not recognize the interplay between heaven and earth. They conceived of time in a very human way, thinking that if consequences hadn't come quickly, they weren't going to come at all.

The wise, on the other hand, don't make this mistake. They see how heaven and earth are deeply intertwined. Instead of resisting God's discipline, they lean into it. They also realize that discipline and judgment are two different things—discipline is corrective, judgment is punitive—and they are willing to learn hard lessons from God. They welcome God's intervention, knowing that their own well-being and society's as a whole will benefit from God stepping into the situation to establish his righteousness.

RE-ENVISION SOCIAL JUSTICE

The psalmist asks who will defend him against the wicked, and the answer is "the LORD" (vv. 16-17). Perhaps one of our greatest missions is to intercede for our cities, our countries, and our world by praying, persistently and in faith, for God to intervene. We can ask him to expose corruption, unravel the work of evildoers, help the helpless, and draw in the marginalized—in other words, to renovate society according to the design of his Kingdom.

Of course, his work in this world is generally done through his people, so remember to envision yourself as at least part of the answer to that prayer. But it's a worthy mission all the way around, from prayer to implementation. You are always on solid ground praying for truth, justice, well-being, provision, integrity, and any other characteristic of a Kingdom of shalom. Appealing to God's own nature—and embodying it—leads to glorious manifestations of his power to save.

Come, let us worship and bow down. Let us kneel before the LORD our maker.

95:6

When the people of Israel complained for lack of water in the wilderness—"though they saw" how God had miraculously provided for them again and again (v. 9)—God made water flow from a rock (Exodus 17:1-7; Numbers 20:1-13). Episodes like this one stuck out in Israel's history as sad examples of their unbelief, for which God was angry with them for forty years (Psalm 95:10). The writer of Hebrews quoted this psalm to urge Jewish Christians not to give up their faith under intense trials (Hebrews 3:7-12). Life with God involves going through some deserts, knowing he will provide help along the way and bring us to the promised place of rest.

In this joyful royal hymn, the psalmist calls God's people to shout joyfully to their Rock of salvation (Psalm 95:1)—a stark contrast to the people's response in the wilderness. He is the King who established the world (vv. 4-5) and Israel (vv. 6-7), and everything belongs to him. He is above all other gods—a truth not taken for granted in Israel, where idolatry was a constant temptation. In light of his majesty, the time to respond to his voice is "today" (v. 7).

RE-ENVISION GOD'S EXTRAVAGANCE

Many Christians, perhaps because of past disappointments, see God as a reluctant miracle-worker; he may use his power in a pinch, but he doesn't want us to rely on it as a way of life. That's not the picture Scripture gives us. The wandering Israelites assumed past miracles were irrelevant to their desperate thirst in the desert, yet God wanted them to ask for his provision again and again. As the writer of Hebrews assures us, God wants us to "come boldly to the throne of grace" in times of need (Hebrews 4:16, NKJV).

That's why Caleb and Joshua were the only members of the Exodus generation to make it into the Promised Land. They had "a different attitude" than others did (Numbers 14:24); they boldly took their Maker at his word. Seeing our Creator as a generous giver overflowing with miraculous gifts is an act of worship—and the reason we can bow before him with joy.

Sing a new song to the LORD! Let the whole earth sing to the LORD!

96:1

A variation of this psalm was sung when David brought the Ark into the Tabernacle to establish Jerusalem as the place of God's presence and Israel's worship center (1 Chronicles 16:23-33). Psalms and the books of Chronicles refer often to worship instruments and worship leaders as far back as David's Tabernacle, continuing through Solomon's Temple, and including Israel's long history into the Captivity and beyond. In contexts of worship, it makes sense for the Ark's journey into Jerusalem, accompanied by David's undignified dancing, to be a prominent and pivotal theme.

The exuberance of this psalm fits that scene. It tells not only Israel but also other nations and creation itself to worship God in his beauty, splendor, majesty, and power. It calls for a "new song" (v. 1) to reflect a new season, a new victory, and a new vision. It's full of hope in God, celebrating the roles he plays throughout history—as Israel's true King, in David's time, and as Israel's Restorer, in the postexilic period (where the Greek version of the Old Testament places it). For us, it pictures the universal reign of God over all other "gods," all governments, and every aspect of our lives.

RE-ENVISION HIS KINGDOM

The church has historically preached the gospel of salvation, but that's only the spiritual core of the gospel of the Kingdom, which is far more prominent in Scripture. The gospel of the Kingdom includes a comprehensive, all-of-life transformation that ends with a new heaven *and* a new earth. Yes, God is "coming to judge the earth" (v. 13), but far beyond rewards and punishments, this judgment involves bringing life, restoring order, establishing justice, and creating harmony under his reign. There is nothing to fear for those who love him; everything that is wrong will be made right.

God almost always involves his people in his work. What role can you play in advancing his Kingdom? Are you just living your life, or do you see yourself on a mission? All of creation to the ends of the earth will one day join in God's restoration. The King has come and will come again, but in many respects he is coming now—through you and all who believe.

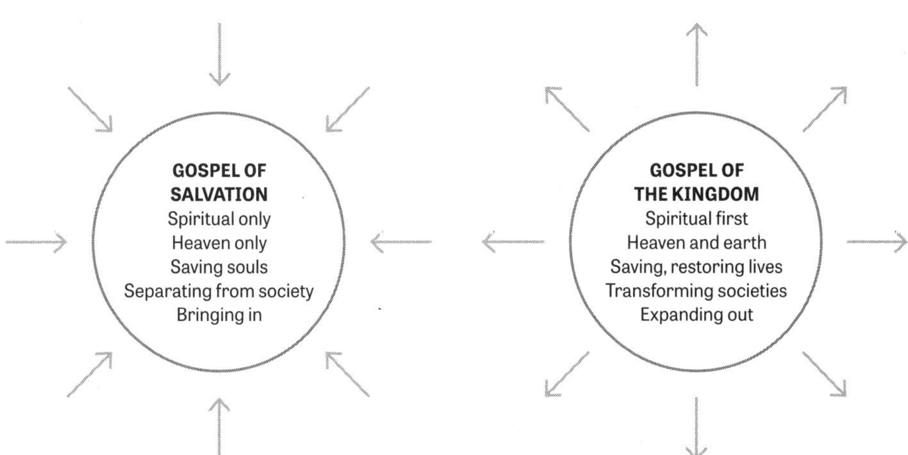

The gospel of salvation is part of the gospel of the Kingdom, but it's not the full picture. The gospel of salvation rightly demonstrates God's love for human beings and his desire for them to spend eternity with him. The gospel of the Kingdom does so, too, but also demonstrates God's goodness and the nature of his Kingdom in this world.

Light shines on the godly, and joy on those whose hearts are right.

97:11

When ancient kings visited the provinces of their kingdom, their processions were designed to make an impression. Here God's entrance makes a much bigger one, as all of nature's strongest forces accompany him. The last verse of the previous psalm announced his coming; here it's shown in highly visual terms.

If this psalm was written during or after the Babylonian exile, as many believe, the psalmist would have been intensely aware of the many gods of dominant cultures—Israel's monotheism was an anomaly in the ancient world. The psalmist would also have been familiar with the immorality and unholy agendas presided over by power-hungry kings. In such a world, a worshiper of Yahweh might have felt greatly outnumbered and isolated—as Daniel and Esther did in those times. Yet the psalmist stayed true to his faith and aligned himself with dramatic scenes of heaven over the visual evidence of earth.

RE-ENVISION YOUR ALIGNMENT

Right now in heaven, thunder and lightning surround God's throne, and multitudes of human and angelic beings sing and shout praises to him (Revelation 4). Meanwhile, we often go about our days as though not much exciting is happening in our lives. Our spirits need to pulsate with the heartbeat of heaven's worship.

It's one thing to rejoice in God as King, another to embrace the full implications by aligning ourselves completely with him. The degree to which you embrace his kingship—not just by agreeing with it but by orienting your life around it and representing his interests—is the degree to which you experience his presence, his joy, and his shalom. Like the psalmist, love righteousness and hate evil (Psalm 97:10), shun worthless idols (v. 7), and rejoice in the Lord (v. 12). Most of all, align your spirit with the awesome scene of the King coming in glory. When "light shines on the godly, and joy on those whose hearts are right," every day is exciting.

The LORD has announced his victory and has revealed his righteousness to every nation!

98:2

According to Paul, creation was subjected to futility and, groaning in expectation, eagerly hopes for its restoration from death and decay (Romans 8:20-22). Even so, the created world still exhibits God's power and divinity, inviting all to learn who he is (Romans 1:20). In the Psalms, creation pours out revelation of God (Psalm 19:1-4) and joins in the song of adoration. When God wins victories, the whole world benefits.

God had "won a mighty victory" with "wonderful deeds" (Psalm 98:1), revealing his righteousness and remembering his promises. This was a victory not just for Israel and the righteousness in Israel's law, but also for "every nation" and "the ends of the earth" (vv. 2-3). If Judah had not been taken captive, it could have remained a relatively isolated kingdom. But as a result of the Captivity—an evil not authored by God but profoundly and dramatically used by him—its people were scattered and planted in faraway places, across Babylon and Persia (and later the Mediterranean Basin). Because of this, God's dealings with them became visible on the international stage. This influence still took centuries to play out, but it all prepared the way for the messianic King who would come.

RE-ENVISION HIS (AND YOUR) RULE

The declaration of Yahweh's kingship is prominent throughout this grouping of psalms. Theologically, we have no trouble with that claim. Practically, we tend to see it as something for the distant future: God *will* reign once all this mess is dealt with, once Jesus returns, and once evil is finally defeated. But in truth, he is King now, over every rival authority, agenda, and argument, revealing himself *through his people*. We are called to see ourselves as the reigning King's children and carry ourselves with a regal attitude and royal authority. God is on his throne, and we are seated next to it with Jesus (Ephesians 2:6). Embrace the enormous honor! Partner with him constantly to advance his Kingdom for you, in you, and through you into the world.

PSALM 99: BETWEEN THE CHERUBIM

He sits on his throne between the cherubim. Let the whole earth quake!

99:1

The Ark of the Covenant was covered with a lid of pure gold with two molded cherubim, one at each end (Exodus 25:17-22). This was the "place of atonement," sprinkled with blood once a year on the Day of Atonement as a covering for Israel's sins (Leviticus 16:14-15). Inside the Ark were the stone tablets God had given Moses and, according to later testimony, Aaron's rod and a pot of manna (Hebrews 9:4), all representing God's presence and power among his people. Above the lid, the "place of atonement" (or "mercy seat"), God would meet with Moses and speak to him.

When the psalmist referred to God's throne "between the cherubim," he was evoking a rich image with multiple connotations regarding God's presence, voice, and mercy. In the context of God receiving praise among "the whole earth" and "all the nations" (vv. 1-2), the image is even more loaded. Wherever the people of Israel and Judah were scattered, God was there. Whichever enemies threatened to capture or destroy, God ruled over them. And to anyone worshiping some false god among the many pagan deities, God would prove himself supreme. In other words, "between the cherubim" may have once been in Jerusalem, but God was both among them—wherever they were—and above all.

RE-ENVISION YOUR REALM

At any given moment, you live at multiple levels in multiple realms, though your vision is likely focused only on the visible world in front of you. But you also exist in a spiritual realm where powers of light and darkness battle, where the spirits of the age compete for the minds and hearts of human beings. And above that, you are seated with Christ in heavenly places (Ephesians 2:6), far above the fray, bearing the authority he so graciously shares with you and trains you by his Spirit to use appropriately. This is where you find his pure presence, his ultimate mercy, and the sound of his voice—"between the cherubim," where he calls you to dwell securely and intimately with him. You do not simply call from earth to heaven; in heavenly realms, you live, pray, and speak to bless the earth.

Enter his gates with thanksgiving; go into his courts with praise. Give thanks to him and praise his name.

100:4

Psalm 100 calls for the whole earth to shout to the Lord with joy. Most of the world doesn't know there's a joy worth shouting about, but there is. We are invited to a lifestyle of worship saturated in gratitude and praise, basking in the presence of God.

In its clearest reading, verse 4 invites us to enter the gates and courts of the Temple—figuratively, God's presence—with thanksgiving and praise. But another way to read it is that thanksgiving and praise are the means by which we enter—in other words, the key to get in. If God is enthroned on the praises of his people (22:3), and his people praise him constantly and passionately, we can see ourselves always existing in his manifest presence. For those who hunger for him, that's an irresistible invitation.

If we merely want to visit God or have him visit us, we'll worship him from time to time. But if we want his habitation rather than just a visitation—to dwell with him and he with us—we will worship constantly. This is more than words, songs, and other expressions of praise. It's a lifestyle. Everything we do can be worship if it's done in faith and with a desire to honor God. Or, as Paul put it, we become living sacrifices as a constant act of worship (Romans 12:1).

RE-ENVISION THE SOUNDTRACK OF YOUR LIFE

The soundtrack or video screen in your mind is going to be filled with something. Usually it's filled with everyday thoughts: to-do lists, relational responsibilities, dreams and desires, and random wanderings. But if it's filled with God-honoring thoughts, expectations of his goodness, visions of his supernatural power, gratitude for what he has already done and what he surely will do—in other words, if you see all of life through God-tinted lenses—you'll find yourself in his courts, where his presence and power overwhelm and transform. This is where life really happens, where everyday thoughts find their answers, and where shouts of joy fill our days.

PSALM 101: A NOBLE CALLING

I will sing of your love and justice, LORD. I will praise you with songs.

101:1

Throughout history, philosophers and dreamers have envisioned the ideal society. Every vision includes concepts like justice and peace, no more ongoing poverty and pain, and wise, good rulers. A good society requires good governance.

That's the vision in this psalm, which serves as an oath or a manifesto for kings in David's dynasty to fulfill. Throughout this vision of godly kingship is an awareness that it can only be accomplished with God's help. Before the king goes about enacting justice in the land, he first sings of God's love and justice as his model (v. 1). He recognizes his need for God—the source of grace and power—for the ability to carry out his pledge (v. 2). He also knows his rule begins at home (vv. 2, 7). Of course, this was not always evident in David's own life, as his home was in chaos for many years. But the psalmist extols the importance of leading "a life of integrity" (v. 2), and he understands that he needs faithful companions (v. 6)—not just friends but like-minded partners to help him build this godly society. These standards are Israel's ideal for the administration of God's truth and reflect messianic expectations.

RE-ENVISION SOCIETY

The king's life is shaped by these commitments, and so are ours. Society is shaped by them too. This is the way it's supposed to be—and the way it will be when the Messiah rules. But the King is looking for faithful companions even now, calling his followers to partner with him in shaping and seasoning society with his truth, justice, and love. If we see ourselves simply as followers of Jesus who are waiting to escape this world, we will never fulfill this calling. If we see ourselves as royal sons and daughters—the princes and princesses of his Kingdom—we can demonstrate, in this age, who he is and what he is like. And we can advance his purposes on earth until he comes. It's a true and noble calling, and it honors the King whose reign we long for.

PSALM 102: AGENTS OF RESTORATION

The children of your people will live in security. Their children's children will thrive in your presence.

102:28

The heading describes this penitential psalm as "a prayer of one overwhelmed with trouble, pouring out problems before the LORD." It's a universal condition; the psalmist could be anyone. He may also be writing on behalf of his people, held captive and exiled from their homeland, longing for the restoration of their city and their kingdom, where God once inhabited his Temple (vv. 12-22). In both contexts, personal and national, life is transient. The psalmist says he is "withering away like grass" (v. 11), and even earth and the heavens will someday "wear out like old clothing" (v. 26). Although he knows God will answer the prayers of the destitute (v. 17), he remains painfully aware of the human condition in a fallen world.

But the human condition and our fallen world are redefined by God and the promises of his Kingdom. He has no end, and therefore his people endure, their children and their children's children thriving in his presence. He restored Jerusalem for the exiles long ago, and he will restore this fallen planet in time. In fact, he is restoring it even now. His people are exhibit A in the restoration project, treasures in earthen vessels (2 Corinthians 4:7, NKJV), growing into the image he gave us, agents of the restoration to come. As transient as our lives were, we are now beautifully everlasting.

RE-ENVISION YOUR LONGEVITY

Perhaps you've envisioned your time running out or longed to break free from the limits of your humanity. From all natural appearances, these are unyielding frustrations that have no solution other than death and the afterlife. But by faith, we are in Christ, and he is eternal. Our work done in faith lasts forever. And future generations continue in his blessing well beyond our lifetime.

This is not fate; you'll need to apply faith for it to be realized. But it's an extravagant invitation to believe, press into the promise, trust God's plan, and rest in his goodness. We and those who follow will thrive in his presence forever.

He fills my life with good things. My youth is renewed like the eagle's!

103:5

About once a year, eagles molt. They lose their feathers, become somewhat weaker in the process, and then soar to new heights with their restored plumage. It's a process of loss and renewal—a concept familiar to the psalmist, the ancient Israelites, and in fact, most human beings. Sometimes when we seem to be fading, we are actually being prepared to reach our peak.

This is the image the psalmist uses to capture the many ways God blesses his people. He begins by talking to his own soul, telling himself to bless the Lord and remember all his benefits. Then he names the benefits: forgiveness of all sins, healing of all diseases, redemption from death, a crown of love and mercy, many "good things," and renewed youth (vv. 3-5). Though this lavish list certainly includes immense spiritual blessings, it is more comprehensive than that. "All" is repeated often. God is interested in our whole lives, not just our spirits, and he meets us at every point of need.

RE-ENVISION THE SCRIPT

This psalm tells us a lot about God, but it also tells us a lot about ourselves. It's an example of how to train ourselves in vision—to rewrite the narrative running through our minds, to refilm the scenes that play out inside of us.

Over the course of our lives, we develop well-worn thought paths that define reality for us. These paths are often wrong, and God wants to replace them with truth. Like the psalmist, we need to talk to our souls and train them to envision reality as God defines it.

Tell your soul what to believe, and don't be shy about believing God's promises. No matter that they seem too extravagant for you; they are promises nonetheless. The more you fill your mouth with praise, the more God fills your life with his presence. That doesn't mean everything instantly becomes easy; clearly it does not. But it does mean everything becomes purposeful and powerful. And as this psalm unequivocally asserts, habitual praise brings God's healing and restoration into every area of our lives.

HALLELUJAH PSALMS

The term *hallelujah* appears in only sixteen psalms and nowhere else in the Old Testament. This may seem surprising because it has been so universally used for centuries in hymns, liturgies, and conversations in multiple languages around the world. Formed from *halelu* (praise) and *yah* (a shortened form of Yahweh), it literally means "praise the Lord" and is generally translated that way in biblical texts. It has become synonymous with other expressions of praise, and we can hardly imagine it not being integral to a vocabulary of faith. Yet its renown comes entirely from the last two books of the Psalter and its repetition in the book of Revelation.

The Hallelujah Psalms include 104–106; 111–118; 135–136; and 146–150. All of these except 104–106 are in Book 5. The word increases in frequency in Book 5, climaxing in the last five psalms of the Psalter. Yet, calls to praise God are far more frequent than the occurrence of this word, and examples fill the pages of Scripture. In fact, this is what many heavenly beings are doing all the time.

Scripture also uses *halelu* apart from *yah,* as well as other words for "praise" that variously mean kneel, bless, honor, and glorify. But as the Psalms come to a close, the repeated "hallelujahs" reinforce the imperative and give the Psalms a resounding unity. This is the chorus of the universe, and we're called to join in with everything in us.

PSALM 104: THE BREATH OF LIFE

When you give them your breath, life is created, and you renew the face of the earth.

104:30

Once again telling his own soul to bless God, the psalmist praises him for all he has done—this time with a focus on creation. It's a reflection of Genesis 1 and the foundation of this world through the creative hands of God, marveling at all he has made. Long ago, God took an earth that was formless and void and made it into something beautiful. He breathed into dust and gave life to it. From disorder to order, emptiness to beauty, lifelessness to life, all was given meaning and purpose.

God's creative energies and renewing breath didn't end there, of course. Humanity fell, corruption and death entered in, and the long story of redemption and restoration began. But in God's mind, it began even earlier, "before the foundation of the world" (Ephesians 1:4, NKJV). He had always planned to breathe his Spirit into human beings and sustain them with his life forever. And he promises a new heaven and a new earth to succeed the old. In God's presence, everything is always being made new.

RE-ENVISION YOUR RENEWAL

Try to envision the vastness of the universe—how a million earths could fit inside the sun, how some five billion suns could fit inside the largest known star, and then how all the galaxies containing such mind-boggling realities could fit on God's fingertip. Now envision that incomprehensibly powerful and limitless God inside of you right now, ready to display the wonders of his glory in response to your faith and trust. This is no fanciful imagination; as Scripture repeatedly tells us, it's real.

That's the God who is restoring you, but you won't experience that restoration if you don't embrace it, dwell on it, and envision it daily. Much in your life will try to convince you that this restoration isn't true, but your natural eyes deceive you. Train yourself in this incomprehensible vision. Let God's life-giving power and energy flow. Like the coming heaven and earth, you are being miraculously and beautifully made new.

PSALM 105: UNTIL THE TIME

Until the time came to fulfill his dreams, the LORD tested Joseph's character.

105:19

Like Psalm 96, this one and the next contain sections of the psalm David wrote to accompany the installation of the Ark of the Covenant in Jerusalem's Tabernacle. In fact, the first fifteen verses of Psalm 105 parallel 1 Chronicles 16:8-22. This song of David confirms God's covenant with Abraham and his promises to Israel. The psalm recounts the Israelites' history into Egypt and back out again, from Joseph through the Exodus, and ends with the second utterance of "hallelujah" in the Psalter (the first was in the previous psalm). It's a hymn of gratitude for God fulfilling his promises to his people—with an expectation that he will do so again and again.

At a pivotal point in this psalm is the figure of Joseph, an exemplary case study in how God's promises play out. God gave Joseph dreams about his future, yet for much of his life, everything seemed to be moving away from those dreams. He was sold into slavery, imprisoned unjustly, and forgotten by someone who promised to help him out. He could have entertained numerous questions about God's promises and faithfulness and about his own faith and actions—and he probably did. Indeed, this psalm says literally that God's word tested him in the process (v. 19; see NKJV). That's what God's promises do. The gap between promise and fulfillment stretches us, disorients us, and nearly undoes us until fulfillment comes. But gloriously, it does come.

RE-ENVISION YOUR DREAMS

If you're living in the gap between promise and fulfillment—and most of us are, most of the time—you may have felt that tension. Learn to see it not as a delay or deferral but as a journey of faith that will certainly end well. Cultivate your spiritual vision during that time, and do not be discouraged by the contradictions you see. The eyes of faith see beyond them. God's history with his people—corporately and individually—is a testimony to his faithfulness. If God has planted dreams in your heart, he will bring them to pass in time.

PSALM 106: FAITH IN THE END

Let me share in the prosperity of your chosen ones. Let me rejoice in the joy of your people; let me praise you with those who are your heritage.

106:5

The previous psalm recounted much of Israel's history to demonstrate God's faithfulness. This one recounts much of Israel's history to demonstrate the people's unfaithfulness. It includes a full confession—the repentance of the psalmist on behalf of his people past and present—and sends a powerful message: *Don't make those mistakes again!* At a time when God's people had been disciplined, lived in exile, and longed for the full restoration of their kingdom and all the promises that came with it, faithfulness was imperative. They did not want their generation to miss out on its promised land too.

So the heart of this psalm is a confession of sin—which we're allowed to do on behalf of our families, communities, or even nations (see Nehemiah 1:4-11; Daniel 9:4-19)—and a plea to share in the prosperity and blessings of God's chosen people. It's one of many reminders that no matter what we've done, how we've failed, or who we've offended, God's plans and purposes allow for redirection and reentry. In fact, God incorporates our failures into his plans, just as he had already compensated for the sins of the patriarchs and Israel long before they happened. His promises took those sins into account. He knew how the people would wander and still promised the destination anyway.

RE-ENVISION YOUR PATH

Perhaps you see your life as a series of missteps and shortcomings. Maybe you're hoping that you haven't forfeited God's purposes and promises along the way. What if all those failures were actually, in the long run, victories? What if you get to the end and hear God say, "You did not let those setbacks destroy you, and you finished the race with faith. Well done!" You may see your failures as hindrances and deal-breakers, but God sees them as testimonies of what you've overcome. Embrace his vision and rejoice in your story's outcome. You can already rejoice in the joy of his people.

BOOK 5: PSALMS 107–150

Enemies and exile are both evident at various points in the last book of Psalms, but so is the fullness of God's Kingdom. In these lines, and sometimes between them, Jerusalem and the Temple are being rebuilt and worship is being restored for God's people. There was a time when songs of Zion could be sung only while in exile in a distant land (see 137:4), but in most of these psalms, they can now be sung in Zion. These hopes and praises crescendo as the Psalter reaches its finale: five psalms filled with "hallelujah."

God is praised in this book for his kindness and compassion for those in need, his brilliance and artistry in creating this world, the strength and protection he offers his people, and his majesty and glory as King of the universe. All heaven and earth, everything that literally or figuratively has breath, including all people everywhere, are called to praise him with songs, dancing, shouts, and all the exuberance a soul can muster.

BACKGROUND

These psalms leave us with a call to perpetual praises, but they also tell us much about how Israel incorporated the worship of Yahweh into their lives. During much of their history as a nation, their worship was lacking—the books of Kings and Chronicles and numerous prophetic warnings make that clear. But in the time of restoration from exile, they discovered a renewed focus and vision for worship.

After captivity, a centuries-old tradition was resurrected. The people of Judah—who once again identified themselves as Israelites—began to make regular pilgrimages to Jerusalem for its annual feasts: Pesach (Passover), Shavuot (Harvest or Weeks), and Sukkot (Shelters or Tabernacles). The Psalms of Ascent (Psalms 120–134; see "Psalms of Ascent" on page 277) capture the anticipation of these journeys, as pilgrims turned their focus to Zion—God's Kingdom as epitomized by his people in Jerusalem and his dwelling place in their Temple. These were culture-shaping moments for a people called to honor their God and his covenant with them.

THE BIG PICTURE

Book 5 is as diverse as any in the Psalter, but three themes express the renewed vision of the editor(s) who compiled and organized these psalms, reorienting our vision to our reason for being and God's ultimate purposes.

The first is *the pursuit of shalom*. We typically translate *shalom* as "peace," but as we've seen throughout the Psalms, it includes much more than our English word *peace* expresses. It's the fullness, wholeness, completeness, abundance, and satisfaction of life as God's people. One psalmist urges prayer for the shalom of Jerusalem and shalom for the people within its walls (122:6-8), but we can assume this is God's will for all who believe in him everywhere. When we live out of sync with him, this interrupts our shalom; his redemption and restoration bring us back into it. *This is the inheritance of his people.*

The second is *the blessing of Aaron* (see Numbers 6:24-26). Hints of that blessing often make their way into these psalms, especially the Psalms of Ascent, and again it is meant for all God's people everywhere. The blessing calls for God's "face to shine upon [us]" (Numbers 6:25, ESV), his grace to fill our lives, and for him to restore our peace—shalom. As priests of our God (Exodus 19:6;

1 Peter 2:9; Revelation 1:6), we have an invitation in the Psalms (and elsewhere) to bless others with God's goodness and grace. *This is the mission of his people.*

The last is *the priority of praise*. This is the biggest picture of all. The greatest commandment is to love God with everything in us (Matthew 22:36-38), and the Psalms repeatedly urge us, invite us, even plead with us to direct our worship to God alone—not because he demands it but because if we really saw clearly, we'd have no other response. When we fill our eyes with a true picture of his magnificence, praise becomes spontaneous. That's the goal of all the images and stories the Psalms give us, and if we want to align ourselves with the ultimate purpose of the universe, it's our goal too. *This is the calling of his people*, and there is none higher.

Has the LORD redeemed you? Then speak out! Tell others he has redeemed you from your enemies.

107:2

Book 4 ends with a prayer for God to gather his people from the nations. Book 5 begins with a hymn of gratitude that he has done so, an echo of the praise that accompanied the procession of the Ark into Jerusalem centuries earlier (see 1 Chronicles 16:34). It's another rehearsal of Israel's history, this time to remember all the ways God has been faithful. Instead of big events like the Exodus and the journey to the Promised Land, it more generally covers the experiences of those in trouble: wanderers in the wilderness (but God "satisfies the thirsty and fills the hungry with good things," Psalm 107:9), the imprisoned (but God breaks their bars, v. 16), the sick (but God heals them, v. 20), those in distress on the seas (but he calms the storms, v. 29), and the poor and hungry (but he rescues them and increases their families, v. 41). In all the trials and tribulations of God's people, he was there for them.

One of the best ways to keep his faithfulness at the forefront of our minds is to speak out about our testimonies (v. 2). Or, as other versions say, "Let the redeemed of the LORD say so" (NKJV, ESV). Those who are wise look back over their history—personal and communal—and intentionally notice God's faithful love (v. 43). In other words, they choose the lens they look through.

RE-ENVISION HIS FAITHFULNESS

Not everyone knows we can make that choice. Some people believe their thoughts are inevitable, not a choice. They become biased toward whatever has gone wrong—all the good things that didn't happen, or the bad things that did—and they grow bitter. But we can instead look back and see God's faithfulness—the good things he did, the bad things he prevented, and how he has walked with us every step of the way. Our view of the past has a remarkable impact on our view of the present and the future—and our moods, expectations, hope, and faith. When "the redeemed of the LORD say so," his reputation flourishes, and so does our joy.

PSALM 108: A CONFIDENT HEART

My heart is confident in you, O God; no wonder I can sing your praises with all my heart!

108:1

Psalm 108 is a compilation from two others: five verses from Psalm 57 and eight from Psalm 60. But it leaves out much of the drama and despair of those psalms. Here the focus is on hope and restoration, likely a product of the postexilic community—the captives who returned to Jerusalem and were restoring their city and Temple. The blessings of David's kingdom are evident in this repurposed praise, but the deep and desperate conflicts are not. This is an occasion for rejoicing in God's deliverance and a prayer for continued favor.

Like many psalms, this is a study in hope. We don't always have hope because we see and believe things that don't stir it up. If we really understood that God is working out everything for our good (Romans 8:28), answering our prayers before we see the answers (see Mark 11:24), and establishing us like fruitful trees by the river (Psalm 1:3), we would rest easy and be filled with joy. If we lose sight of those (and many other) assurances, we become weighed down and deflated. A true vision causes our spirits to rise up in hope.

RE-ENVISION YOUR CORE BELIEFS

If you aren't overflowing with hope in a situation, dig down to discover what you actually believe about it. If your heart lacks confidence in God, explore why. Is it past experiences, present circumstances, or future uncertainties? Our natural sight can be very persuasive on these things. But eyes of faith choose a better view that is filled with God and permeated with his promises. When we really see who he is and really believe what he says, our hearts become sure, our mouths are filled with heartfelt praise (Psalm 108:1), and we live with anticipation that "we will do mighty things" (v. 13) with his help, for his glory, and always for our good.

PSALM 109: THE SERPENT AND THE SEED

He stands beside the needy, ready to save them from those who condemn them.

109:31

This world is entrenched in a conflict that natural eyes can't see. Yet the evidence of battle is there, written into the stories of our times and the wounds of our hearts. It has been cast as good versus evil, light versus dark, wisdom versus ignorance, and the sacred versus the profane. More specifically, it's God putting down a rebellion that began in heavenly realms and caught up all of earth in its defiance. Yet, for now, God is letting it run its course for greater purposes—the revelation of who he is, the distinction between those who love him and those who don't, the redemption of all who follow him, and the restoration of heaven and earth into something greater than before.

These are the times of deep and dreadful enmity, which go back to our origins (Genesis 3:15). The enmity between the serpent and the Seed—Satan's offspring and Eve's—is reflected in the words of this psalm. Whether the curses of verses 6-19 are the voice of David against his accusers or the accusers against David isn't clear in the original text, but in either case, this psalm pits the anointed king (David) against his archenemy. Behind the scenes in the cosmic war, we can see the Anointed King against his archenemy, Satan (literally "accuser"). The conflict is deep and intense, the words harsh, and the judgments severe. This is the animosity that, one way or another, tears the world apart.

RE-ENVISION YOUR DEFENSE

In this war-torn world, you have an irrefutable advocate. He defends you against the Accuser and vindicates you in the end. You play a part in your own defense; you overcome the Accuser by the blood of the Lamb and the word of your testimony (Revelation 12:11). But in any trial you go through, you need to see your advocate beside you and feel his strength within you. The conflict will continue to rage, but your heart can be at peace. He is always ready to save.

MESSIANIC PSALMS

The kings of Israel and Judah—including the united kingdom's first king, Saul, who did not live up to his calling—were considered "anointed." The Hebrew word for "anointed" (*mashiach*) is where we get the word *Messiah* (literally, "anointed one"). And in a sense, all kings appointed by God had some sort of a messianic calling to rule their society as God's Kingdom. The people may not have viewed all these kings in terms of messianic expectations, and many of the kings didn't live up to the calling. But David certainly came to be viewed that way, and he became the "type" (or foreshadowing) of the messianic King to come. Throughout the history of Israel and Judah, many among God's people looked for a true Son of David to rule them—a descendant with the heart of David (but not his flaws) who would restore the kingdom forever.

This interplay between anointed kings and messianic expectations is evident in many of the psalms, including Psalms 2, 16, 18, 20–22, 45, 69, 72, 110, and 118. Some of the royal psalms (see "Royal Psalms" on page 215) refer specifically to the anointed king. Other psalms came to be seen as messianic over time because of their unusual wording (for example, Psalm 110) or because of changed expectations of the future. Others came to be viewed as messianic in retrospect because of how they describe the Messiah's suffering. In most of these psalms, the context is clearly the Davidic covenant—God's promise to make David's kingdom everlasting (2 Samuel 7:16). The psalmists surely did not know the full implications of their Spirit-inspired words or how they would unfold centuries later, but they knew the kind of kingdom God wanted to establish because they knew the nature of the King.

Many prophets and psalmists cast a vision for what that Kingdom might look like. Scripture gives us an open invitation to continue this by envisioning that Kingdom and anticipating it with joy. Even more, we have been commissioned by the messianic King. We are called to pray for that Kingdom to come, cultivate its character within us, and let it overflow into the world around us. Our gatherings are to be Kingdom outposts, each of us a resident ambassador establishing the influence of the King in a foreign land. The Messiah came and is coming again. In between, he works through his people to further his Kingdom mission on earth.

The LORD will extend your powerful kingdom from Jerusalem; you will rule over your enemies.

110:2

The first verse of this messianic prophecy was quoted by Jesus himself (Matthew 22:41-46). It's the most often-quoted Old Testament verse in the New Testament because it reveals the future reign of the messianic King. Its language is surprising—"Yahweh" spoke to "Adonai," portrayed here as two figures, with both being Lord over David. This son of David, the messianic King, would be a priest forever in the order of Melchizedek. Melchizedek was the priest-king of Salem (the same root word as *shalom*), that is, Jerusalem. He once gave Abraham bread and wine, blessed him, and received his tithe (Genesis 14:18-20). David could hardly have imagined the monumental fulfillment of his words in this psalm, but the writer of Hebrews did (Hebrews 7). David's enemies—and God's—would be subdued. This includes those who made such vicious accusations as recounted in the prior psalm.

The king not only rules over his enemies but, as verse 2 says, literally, "in the midst of them" (see, for example, NKJV). The enemies are still there, but they have been stripped of their power—a gratifying picture for participants in that reign (see Revelation 3:21; 5:10). We can hold on to this image, remembering that we will one day sit victoriously with Christ on his throne, even as we contend for his Kingdom here and now. We are called not only to follow Jesus but also to represent him in the midst of conflict and opposition. There's no need to be intimidated by the presence of our enemies. We can flourish there. This is the Messiah's mission in our age, and we get to be a part of it.

RE-ENVISION YOUR ENEMIES

Many Christians see themselves as being "under" the worldly and spiritual oppressors around them. Few can see the bigger picture or recognize the unfounded intimidation by powers in the process of losing their grip. The early church thrived in such conditions, and we can too. Even as the battle rages, we have ample opportunities to reflect the character and nature of the Anointed King, subduing his enemies' evil, hatred, and lies with his goodness, love, and truth. When we see his enemies as his footstool—even before his return, while he is still seated at the Father's right hand (Psalm 110:1)—we live with the boldness, authority, and peace we were meant to have.

PSALM 111: THE ULTIMATE PROMISED LAND

He has shown his great power to his people by giving them the lands of other nations.

111:6

As the prior psalm declares, the Son reigns. Six of the next seven psalms lift up their "hallelujah," this one in the first word. In its original context, the psalm reflects a shift away from Temple sacrifices and toward the wisdom of Torah observance (vv. 9-10)—a necessary development during the Exile, when the Temple was in ruins and captives clung to the revelation God had given them long before. This psalm celebrates that covenant and its instructions, as the psalmist marvels that God gave his people the land of other nations in Joshua's day (v. 6). Returned exiles hoped for God to confirm and perpetuate his reign in Israel and for his people to respond by fearing him and living out the wisdom they had once been given (v. 10).

From a New Testament perspective, we see the language of this psalm more prophetically. Because the Son (and his followers) was invited to ask for the nations as an inheritance (Psalm 2:8), and because Jesus sends his disciples to the ends of the earth to make disciples of all nations (Matthew 28:18-20), we envision a salvation that reaches far beyond Israel, with people from all nations and languages worshiping God (Revelation 7:9-10). The whole world is his, and he shares it with his people.

RE-ENVISION THE EARTH

In strongly visual language, the prophet Habakkuk invites us to see God's glory covering the earth "as the waters cover the sea" (Habakkuk 2:14, ESV). Other psalms call for all nations to worship him (117:1) and for the whole earth to be filled with his glory (72:19). In other words, if we aren't filled with a global vision, we're underestimating God and missing at least part of our calling. Inhabited by his Spirit, you are among the waves of glory covering the earth; as an intercessor, you play a role in their continuing spread. It's a promised land of epic proportions, and you are instrumental in entering it.

How joyful are those who fear the LORD and delight in obeying his commands.

112:1

This psalm is a twin of the last one, similar in theme and structure (they are both acrostics). Both psalms bear common phrases, such as "his righteousness endures forever," which is the literal translation of verse 3 in each psalm. The benefits of fearing the Lord and delighting in his commands are enormous: successful children (v. 2), prosperity and lasting works (v. 3), lives full of light (v. 4), protection from evil (v. 6), fearlessness (v. 8), and influence and honor (v. 9). It's an expansive promise that sums up many of the blessings applied to the wise in Proverbs. This takes the declarations of Psalm 1 to another level.

It is said that Psalm 111 is a portrait of the Lord and Psalm 112 a portrait of the believer.* The connections between the two portraits are striking. Both are righteous, enduring, gracious, and merciful; established and remembered forever; and just and truthful. It makes sense that God's children would be like their Father; he fills us with his Spirit, instructs us in his ways, and conforms us to his image, as we were designed to be. The result is joy—for him and us.

RE-ENVISION FEAR

The idea of fearing the Lord while delighting in his commands may seem dissonant, but Scripture often blends both attitudes freely, including in this

* Michael Wilcock, *The Message of Psalms 73–150: Songs for the People of God*, BST (Downers Grove, IL: IVP Academic, 2002), 172.

psalm and throughout Proverbs. On the one hand, God holds his people in his arms and sings tenderly to them (Zephaniah 3:17). On the other hand, people who see him fall down as though dead (Ezekiel 1:28; Revelation 1:17). He is at once awe-inspiring and intimate, and we have to learn to see both sides at once. Envisioning one to the exclusion of the other breeds either the wrong kind of fear or casual familiarity. But delight and fear together invite the fullness of his presence and power to dwell within us. We take on his nature, do his works, and enjoy his fellowship forever.

EGYPTIAN HALLEL

Psalms 113–118 form the "Egyptian Hallel" (also called "Passover Hallel"). These praises were written during the reconstruction period to be sung at the Passover meal and other feasts. They reflect on Israel's redemptive history, referring back to captivity in Egypt and the Exodus (114:1). For former exiles returning to Jerusalem from Babylonian captivity, this was a highly relevant and encouraging theme. After all, in the past God had miraculously accomplished one exodus for his people; this return was another.

Hallel simply means "praise," and these psalms are full of it. They respond to God's deliverance and love and reflect the restored community's ideals: fruitfulness where they were once barren, care for the oppressed and needy, a rejection of idolatry, and God's blessing on the congregation and its priests. Not coincidentally, this group of psalms is followed immediately by a strong emphasis on the Torah (Psalm 119), which would come to characterize the restored community perhaps more than any other feature. These are songs not only of deliverance but also of a renewed vision.

That makes them particularly relevant to the Passover meal, which originated in Israel's exodus from Egypt and journey toward the Promised Land. Jesus and the disciples sang at their last supper together (Mark 14:26), and their hymns most likely came from this collection. Psalms 113–114 were (and are) traditionally sung before the Passover meal, while Psalms 115–118 are sung after. The psalmists who wrote them could hardly have envisioned the deliverance and renewed vision that would follow that evening before the Crucifixion, but we can. And we can join in these praises with the expectation of fulfillment and the fullness of joy they point to.

PSALM 113: RAGS TO RICHES

He stoops to look down on heaven and on earth. He lifts the poor from the dust.

113:6-7

The postexilic community saw themselves as poor, needy, and barren (vv. 7, 9). Many of their families were once well-off and influential in Judah before the Babylonian captivity, but exile has a way of leveling the social landscape. Those who returned to Jerusalem to rebuild it had a long struggle in front of them. Those who remained in the cities of Persia faced an ongoing struggle as minorities in a foreign land. The people of God had, by his design, been brought low.

But their suffering was not pointless. They had been brought low for a purpose, and that included ultimately being built back up—as those who read the Prophets now knew. So with this in mind, they appealed to God's generous nature. He always shows compassion for the poor, needy, and barren. No matter how high in heaven he stands, he is always willing to stoop low to rescue his people on earth (v. 6). And it is always more than a rescue. God replaces the shame of his people with honor, their poverty with wealth, and their frustration with fulfillment. He even places paupers among princes (v. 8). He is the original author of rags-to-riches stories.

RE-ENVISION YOUR STORY

In one way or another, we are all a rags-to-riches story. Regardless of the circumstances we come from, the spiritual landscape leveled us, and we desperately needed God's help. As he did with Hannah (whose song in 1 Samuel 2 is quoted here in vv. 7-8), he replaces our barrenness with lasting fruitfulness. He doesn't just solve our problems; he lifts us up into places of favor and honor. We are children of the King, princes and princesses who were once paupers, a royal priesthood commissioned to stand in the gap between God and humanity to bring more heirs into the Kingdom. If that's not how you see your story, work on your vision. Know who you are. You have been lifted up and set in the highest places there are.

PSALM 114: WHEN NATURE BENDS

Tremble, O earth, at the presence of the Lord, at the presence of the God of Jacob.

114:7

To the exiles scattered across Persian lands, the long period of restoration was like a second Exodus. Just as their ancestors had been led out of Egypt hundreds of years earlier, now they were being led out of a foreign land belonging to people of a "strange language" (v. 1; see ESV and NKJV), returning to their past and future Promised Land. No matter that many no longer understood Hebrew like their parents did; they were going home.

Psalm 114 celebrates that long-ago redemption from Egypt to the Promised Land, not only because it was such a miraculous founding event in Israel's history but also because it reminded them that God could do it again. That's always how his miracles work; past wonders serve as invitations for us to trust him for present ones. And in the long century of return—the books of Ezra and Nehemiah record numerous waves of return over many years—the Israelites needed to focus their faith on the God who had always accomplished great things on their behalf.

So the psalmist teasingly laughs at the seas, rivers, and mountains that, against the laws of physics, bowed to God's agenda. The Red Sea, the Jordan River, the mountains, even a rock that turned into a spring of water—all of creation gives way to God's redemptive plan. If Jesus sang this song at the

Passover meal, which seems likely, it pointed directly toward the exodus he was about to accomplish. Nothing, not even death, can prevent God from fulfilling his promises to his people.

RE-ENVISION YOUR OBSTACLES

Perhaps you've seen the obstacles in your way as unyielding and cruel. If you've focused on them long enough, they may even seem bigger than God, or at least like they have a stronger will. But as past miracles have shown us, nothing can get in God's way when he's ready to deliver. Even the obstacles serve him and highlight his supernatural power. Feel free to laugh at them like the psalmist does. When God has made a promise to his people, he will move heaven and earth to fulfill it.

PSALM 115: THE IMAGE WE HONOR

Those who make idols are just like them, as are all who trust in them. O Israel, trust the LORD! He is your helper and your shield.

115:8-9

The returned exiles were well aware of why they (and in most cases, their parents and grandparents) had been living in a foreign land. The prophets had made it very clear. The Exile was a result of their disobedience. The people of Judah had broken their covenant with God—not just once but over hundreds of years, through injustice, corruption, and especially idolatry. In fact, idolatry was at the root of it all, a violation of Israel's most fundamental commandment to love the Lord with all their heart, soul, and strength (Deuteronomy 6:5). Of all the commandments they broke, this was the root source of rebellion.

So this psalm, written during the period of restoration, emphatically denounces idols as empty, impotent, and pointless (vv. 4-8). Mere objects, no matter how valuable, can give no revelation, make no promises, accomplish no miracles, and save no lives. God is in heaven and can do whatever he wishes (v. 3), and he wishes to bless his people and give them the land/earth (vv. 12-16). For that (and many other reasons), he is worthy of praise.

As for those who make and trust idols, they grow into the image they worship (v. 8). We always conform to what we love. Idolatry dulls the senses and deadens the spirit because idols are senseless and dead. Only God can fill us with life, vision, and understanding.

RE-ENVISION YOUR ATTACHMENTS

Be careful what you worship. Ostensibly, that's God; few people today have human-made idols in their homes. But idols such as wealth, popularity, beauty, and power can linger in the depths of our hearts, and if we honor and entertain them, we start to be consumed by them. Whatever grips your vision, captures your imagination, occupies your thoughts, and otherwise fills your days can shape you in powerful ways. That's why it's so important to live a Spirit-saturated life. Envision his marvelous, miraculous works flowing to you and through you. He is the only attachment worthy of your worship. Let him fill you with his wisdom, power, and love.

Let my soul be at rest again, for the LORD has been good to me.

116:7

Paul once wrote of being "delivered to death for Jesus' sake" so that the life of Jesus might be made manifest in him (2 Corinthians 4:7-15, NKJV). We have a priceless treasure within our earthly vessels—our bodies—and our life in Christ involves making that treasure visible, sometimes accomplished amid physical suffering. So Paul was not alarmed if his body was wasting away; it only made God's power more obvious. In that context of his repeated close calls with death, he quoted this psalm: "I believed in God, so I spoke" (2 Corinthians 4:13; Psalm 116:10). It's a small phrase loaded with an invitation to cry out to God whenever we're in trouble.

It's likely that Jesus sang this hymn after the Passover meal (Mark 14:26). With its numerous allusions to being rescued from death (vv. 3, 6, 8, 16), this psalm carried meaning beyond what the psalmist could have imagined. There was no greater crisis in human history than the Savior of the world being placed in a tomb. When the stone sealed the opening, all hope seemed lost. Yet that crisis set the stage for the greatest, most absolute deliverance the world could ever know. Deliverance was a theme precious to the Israelites throughout their history—from Egypt to the Promised Land to Babylon and back again. But each of those rescues was temporary; the exodus Jesus accomplished lasts forever.

RE-ENVISION HOPE

There will be times when your vision is filled with obstacles, threats, dreadful events, oppressive circumstances, and even the prospect of death. You will see them right in front of you, and you'll face a choice. You can let them define your experience, or you can lift the veil from your spiritual eyes and see the God beyond them. One choice leads to hopelessness, the other to hope. The hopelessness is a lie, but the hope is the truest truth there is. Embrace it, let the Spirit of God fill you with it (Romans 15:13), and let your soul return to rest.

PSALM 117: EVERYBODY EVERYWHERE

Praise the LORD, all you nations. Praise him, all you people of the earth.

117:1

This shortest of psalms presents one theme, but it's a big one. It envisions all nations (in Hebrew, the *goyim*)—pagan peoples across the earth—praising the Lord. This includes Israel's enemies: the Egyptians who once held the Israelites captive, the peoples in and around Canaan who were antagonists in Israel's early national history, the Babylonians who took Judah captive, and the Persians with whom many remained intermingled after the return. This vision even looks beyond these familiar nations to unknown places in the world.

This hymn was among those traditionally sung after the Passover meal in Jesus' time (and often today), and it has huge implications in following a psalm about deliverance from death. It looks ahead, prophetically encompassing the post-Resurrection commission Jesus gave his disciples: to go into the world and disciple all nations (Matthew 28:18-20; Mark 16:15; Luke 24:47; Acts 1:8). Paul quoted Psalm 117:1 in Romans 15:11 as one of several pieces of evidence that God always intended to include Gentiles in his plan. Believers are called to go into all the world in resurrection power, sharing the good news of the Kingdom so all nations can enter into it.

RE-ENVISION MISSIONS

These two brief verses also point to the ultimate purpose of missions: praising God for his unfailing love. As John Piper put it, "Missions exists because worship doesn't." Our goal is to bring all peoples "into the white-hot enjoyment of God's glory."* We aren't just trying to get people saved. We want them to enter a fulfilling, satisfying, joyful relationship with God in which they experience the wholeness of his shalom and overflow with praises to him in response. Our greatest testimony is our joy in him! We are carriers not just of his message but also of his goodness, his wisdom, his power, and his love in every area of life. In whatever ways he displays himself in us and through us, we are missionaries to the world.

* John Piper, *Let the Nations Be Glad!: The Supremacy of God in Missions* (Grand Rapids, MI: Baker Academic, 1993), 11.

PSALM 118: GOD OUR HELPER

The LORD is for me, so I will have no fear. What can mere people do to me?

118:6

Israel, and specifically the people of Judah returning from exile, had been through all sorts of ups and downs and twists and turns throughout their history. Much of their trouble was of their own making, but it was traumatic regardless of the source. Yet through it all, and with a new era dawning, they could still say repeatedly "his faithful love endures forever" (vv. 1-4, 29)—the same declaration that marked the laying of the foundation for the new Temple during this time (Ezra 3:11). Israel's experiences might have been all over the map, literally and figuratively, but God's love for them never changed.

This psalm is full of landmark verses. Jesus quoted Psalm 118:22-23 to depict himself as the "the cornerstone" that was rejected by the supposed builders of God's Kingdom (Matthew 21:42). God's people have long sung joyfully, "This is the day the LORD has made. We will rejoice and be glad in it" (Psalm 118:24). And the writer of Hebrews encouraged his intimidated readers with the words of verse 6 about having no fear (Hebrews 13:6). Though surrounded by human accusers, we can remember that God, our helper, is in the same picture. Because of this, we can live with complete confidence—a fact that provoked enthusiastic praise from the psalmist.

RE-ENVISION YOUR HELP

When Elisha's servant was alarmed to see enemy warriors, horses, and chariots surrounding their camp, Elisha prayed that God would open the servant's eyes. Suddenly he saw even greater armies of angels and chariots of fire surrounding the enemies (2 Kings 6:15-17). The psalmist could relate; though surrounded by hostile forces (vv. 10-13), he saw God as his strength and sang songs of victory (vv. 14-16).

When we lift our gaze from the enemies or obstacles vying for our attention and instead look to the God who is our constant helper, we become fearless. We rejoice in the day he has made—every day. We experience every blessing of this psalm through the vision it gives us. And because we stand as testimonies of his faithful love that endures forever, others will experience his blessings too.

PSALM 119: IMMERSED IN TRUTH

Your decrees have been the theme of my songs wherever I have lived.

119:54

This longest of psalms (and longest chapter in the Bible) is the preeminent Torah psalm. God's Word—commandments, statutes, instructions, testimonies, precepts, ways, laws, and so on—is depicted through eight different Hebrew words, all of which represent the Torah or law of Moses. Of course, God's Word extends beyond the Torah proper into the Prophets (*Nevi'im*) and Writings (*Ketuvim*). But the centerpiece, the foundation of Israel's faith, remains the Torah, the Pentateuch, the five books from Genesis to Deuteronomy. And here it is honored in a multitude of ways, including the psalm's memorable acrostic structure, to impress upon readers the primacy of God's Word.

In the rebuilding of Jerusalem and the homeland, it makes sense that Israel would prioritize recommitting themselves to the law and instructing young people in it. After all, it was negligence of the law that had led to their downfall and captivity. And, as recent history had shown, a temple could be destroyed, and even when standing, it could exist only in one place. God's Word could always be everywhere. It keeps God's sheep within the borders of his pasture, but it's far better than a guardrail. It becomes a gateway into his pastures we have not yet seen. It's an invitation into all the riches and depths of his Kingdom.

RE-ENVISION THE WORD

In our rationalist age, we tend to view Scripture as something to learn. Scripture itself certainly supports learning, but it redefines it for us. The Bible is far more than an instruction manual for life. We don't just receive information from it. We immerse ourselves in it, absorb it, envision it, wear it, embody it, become it, and exude it. Some even "eat" it and find that it tastes "sweeter than honey" (Psalm 119:103; Ezekiel 3:1-3; see also Revelation 10:9-10). This immersion is the heart of God's instructions in Deuteronomy 6:6-9. For us today, with a more expansive Scripture than ancient Israel had, it's even more transforming. Jesus, the Word made flesh, implants his Spirit within us to put flesh on it too. See the Word as the fabric of your life and wear it well.

PSALMS OF ASCENT

In many ways, the history of Israel—and of God's people in general—is a journey. The founding patriarch journeyed to the land God would show him (Genesis 12:1, 4). Israel's namesake wrestled with God on his journey back from years in his mother's homeland (Genesis 32). The captives of Egypt traveled through the Red Sea and across the wilderness into the Promised Land. And after years of exile in Babylonian and Persian lands, the captives journeyed back to that same Land of Promise. It makes sense, then, that every pilgrimage to Jerusalem and its Temple, in any age, would be seen as a representation of a much greater pilgrimage.

The Psalms of Ascent (Psalms 120–134) were written or compiled with pilgrims in mind as they went up to Jerusalem to celebrate Israel's feasts. This collection is also known as the Pilgrim Psalter, gradual psalms, or "step" psalms because they represent stages or steps on that journey, and Levites sang them on the fifteen steps leading from the court of women to the court of Israel in the Temple. Not only were they a fitting accompaniment for the journey to Jerusalem, but they also evoked images of the great pilgrimage out of exile. However they were used, they painted a picture of God's people moving toward his dwelling place.

These psalms include a range of images and topics and are varied in tone. Some are joyful, others plaintive, some instructive, and others filled with pleading. Several include verbiage from Aaron's priestly blessing (Numbers 6:24-26), pronouncing grace and peace on God's people. They celebrate community and especially its gathering at God's house. The central psalm in the collection (Psalm 127) honors both the Temple and Jerusalem while also blessing the work and families of God's people. In short, these are odes to Zion and its God, affirmations that all who journey into the place of his presence are pilgrims headed to their heart's true home.

PSALM 120: IN SEARCH OF SHALOM

I took my troubles to the LORD; I cried out to him, and he answered my prayer.

120:1

The Psalms of Ascent begin with the lament and prayer of someone living in a distant land among people who don't adhere to the covenant and don't have shalom (v. 6). He doesn't fit in. He takes his troubles to the Lord—anyone can do that anytime—but we also get the sense that he wants to take his troubles to Jerusalem. This is not just a journey to a city; it's a journey to the place of God's presence. There he expects to find the shalom he is looking for, where his people inhabit the city and the Lord inhabits his Temple.

The Psalms of Ascent are filled with such hopes. Even when they describe troubling situations, they are tinged with joy and expectation. After a long exile in a foreign land, and in the centuries after, the people of God rejoiced at the privilege of going up to Jerusalem once again. Wherever they were, however far removed they felt from God's presence, however awkward they felt among people who did not know him—a common experience in growing diaspora communities—they lived with an eye toward Jerusalem, the spiritual home of their people and the place of shalom.

RE-ENVISION YOUR LONGINGS

What are you really looking for? Like all of us, you long for rest—perhaps a break from work, a nice vacation, the right home or job, a respite from the chaos and responsibilities of your life, or whatever will give you a sense of peace. But the human heart really longs for a deeper peace, the fullness of shalom, the feeling that all is right in its world. We can find this only in God's presence, and we can find it there even when everything isn't right in our world. He lifts us up above the mess and takes us into his arms, where no disturbance remains. Even better, he fills us with his Spirit so his presence goes with us everywhere. No matter what is going on around you, see yourself in that place—unmovable, undisturbed, and at peace.

He will not let you stumble; the one who watches over you will not slumber.

121:3

Like Psalm 91, this song promises God's protection. In the earlier psalm, the threats were from a battle. Here they are the dangers of the road. But wherever the pilgrim goes, regardless of the terrain or the bandits concealed in it, no matter how hot the sun or how steep the climb, the Lord is watching over him. And unlike the pilgrim's fellow travelers, the divine watchman never sleeps.

On our lifelong journey into (and in) God's presence, we are under the care of the most benevolent and powerful being in the universe. He's not a local deity, he doesn't lose his focus, he isn't too busy to care, and he's not too far above us. He's right there with us, next to us, actively caring for us in everything we go through, even if we don't always sense his presence or his attention. He doesn't remove every obstacle or spare us from every hardship, but neither does he leave us to fend for ourselves. Nothing can touch us that he doesn't allow, even while we sleep.

RE-ENVISION HIS CLOSENESS

Most of us tend to see our problems as "around us" and God as beyond them. We envision our prayers as invitations for him to come into the midst of our problems and help us in times of need. But God tells us he is closer than that. He stands between us and our problems, and they can only get to us through him. So why do they get to us? Perhaps he is training our hands for battle (Psalm 144:1), testing our faith (1 Peter 1:7), disciplining us to get us back on track (Hebrews 12:5-11), drawing us closer as he walks with us through our trials (Isaiah 43:1-2), setting up a display of his character (John 9:3), or allowing us to share in Jesus' sufferings (Philippians 3:10-11). Regardless of the reason, he is there. And nothing can distract or deter him from constantly taking care of us.

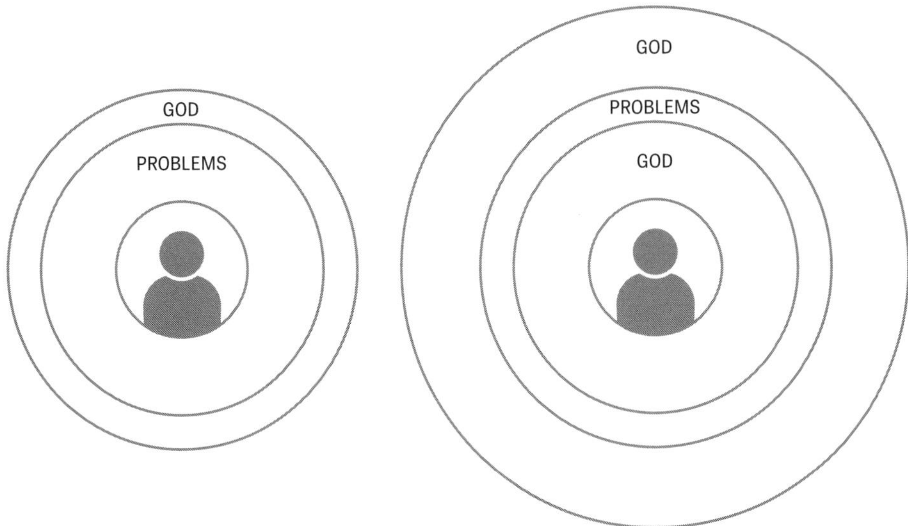

When we see ourselves as surrounded by problems, they create a barrier between us and God, and we pray for him to solve or remove them from a distance. When we see him between us and our problems (as well as above them)—in fact, as dwelling within us through his Spirit—he is a barrier to our problems, and we have faith that he will work for us and through us to resolve them.

PSALM 122: THE HOUSE OF GOD

I was glad when they said to me, "Let us go to the house of the LORD."

122:1

Pilgrims to Jerusalem in any season looked forward to the journey. Their festivals were times of celebration, fellowship, and worship, and they stirred up a sense of common identity. Together they would feast, talk, repent, and remember their collective history and the promises of fulfillment—God's people redeemed, preserved, and destined for a glorious future. They would also pray for the shalom of Jerusalem (vv. 6-8). And they would do all these things in the shadow of the Temple—after it had been rebuilt—where the Promiser and Fulfiller said he would dwell.

We have no such building that serves as God's dwelling place in this way. Our churches are gathering places, not temples. Nor do we have a holy city that draws us to it in pilgrimage. We worship wherever we are, whenever we can. But these ancient symbols of presence and devotion do point us to greater truths. A holy city is under construction—and has been for ages (Hebrews 11:9-10; see also 12:22-24)—and the house of God's presence already exists (1 Corinthians 3:16; 6:19; Ephesians 2:19-22). He is in us, creating and re-creating until the New Jerusalem comes in glory.

RE-ENVISION YOUR PILGRIMAGE

Your life is a journey, and you've probably assumed that your destination is heaven. That's true, but it's more than a place. It's a Person—an identity in Christ, a permanent position in his arms. To go to the house of the Lord, you don't need to travel anywhere. Lean back in him, let his Spirit flow, talk with him in the depths of your spirit, hear his voice, and enjoy the fellowship. Your destination is not out there somewhere in the future. You're there now, and he is too. And when you gather with others in whom he dwells, the joy is magnified many times over. For the sake of the house of the Lord—in you and among you—rejoice in the shalom of his presence.

We keep looking to the LORD our God for his mercy, just as servants keep their eyes on their master.

123:2

One psalmist had declared his need to lift up his eyes, past the mountains, to see the Lord who made heaven and earth and would be his help (121:1). With ample promises of God's protection (121:2-8), he reassured himself. But the psalmist in this song is not interested in a mere lifting of the eyes. This is a fixed gaze, an unflinching plea to the one enthroned above. He understood how the gaze of faith works.

When you're depending on God for some answer and it hasn't come yet, at what point do you stop looking to the Lord and turn to other sources of help? When do you assume God helps those who help themselves? You don't. Just a few psalms ago, a psalmist declared that "all human help is useless" (108:12), at least compared to God's. God may work through other human beings to help us, but he never wants us to depend solely on them. He is the ultimate source for our needs. The eyes of faith have no plan B. They cannot turn away. He is the only real provision.

RE-ENVISION YOUR GAZE

We may not live in a world in which servants look to their masters for a hint of direction or provision, but the picture should not be lost on us. When we depend on God completely and without reservation, we don't turn our gaze away—even when he waits, or we wonder how long, or he stretches us, or we chafe at the testing, or his promises linger beyond our patience. Where else are we going to look? He has the words and ways of life (John 6:66-69). We have nowhere else to go.

When you truly depend on God, you pin all your hopes on him. Trusting hearts see him not as a possible answer but the only one. There are no other options. And hearts that look so purely to him will always receive his mercy.

What if the LORD had not been on our side?

124:1

Counterfactual history is always a shaky proposition. There's no way we can know what would have happened under other circumstances. But we can imagine. Sometimes we know how grateful we ought to be because we can see the alternatives. And if God had not been on our side . . . well, it's painful to think of the dark side of that "if."

For Israel, it likely would have meant ongoing defeat and captivity by other nations and perhaps even the extinction of their people. They might have fared like any other nation that wasn't called to be God's chosen people—there are both blessings and hardships that come with that calling—but faring like other nations is hardly an appealing prospect. In reality, Israel went through many crises, and God delivered them, sometimes miraculously, always with love and an eye toward his everlasting promises. Alternative histories for Israel are hard to imagine. The rhetorical question is best left rhetorical.

But Paul finishes the thought for those who believe: "If God is for us, who can ever be against us?" (Romans 8:31). His rhetorical question has a more concrete answer: no one. When God is on our side, we're invincible. In any situation, he's the deciding factor.

RE-ENVISION THE ALTERNATIVES

When it finally sinks in that God is on your side, everything changes. Your faith does not free you from all conflict; in fact, it brings you to the front lines, and sometimes you suffer losses there. But it gives you meaning, everlasting promises, and a relationship that will sustain you through anything for all time. Your life without him would be something far more traumatic than your life with him. God on your side is always a good deal.

Live with no regrets. The ifs of life without God are all bad. He never promises easy, but he does promise fulfillment. And there's no if about that. He's always on your side.

PSALM 125: HEARTS IN SYNC

O LORD, do good to those who are good, whose hearts are in tune with you.

125:4

The writer of Hebrews talks about the world being shaken so that only unshakable things will remain (Hebrews 12:26-28). While everything is in turmoil around us, while a polarized world casts shame and hatred everywhere, while the possibilities of military, technological, and environmental destruction are talked about regularly, we are planted securely on Mount Zion—not literally in Jerusalem, as the psalmist saw it, but genuinely in the dwelling place of God. Anchored in him, those who trust in the Lord are secure—even among challenges the psalmist could hardly conceive of.

Those who trust in the Lord have tuned their hearts to his. We become like the one we honor, conformed to the image of what or whom we love. If the one we love is immovable, so are we. A heart in sync with his will love what he loves, hate what he hates, grieve where he grieves, and rejoice where he rejoices. That alignment may not end every struggle in our lives, but it does bring peace. Israel's shalom in times of trouble (Psalm 125:5) becomes ours.

RE-ENVISION THE SHAKING

The world is shaking. You've certainly noticed that. The question is whether you are shaking with it. Do you see yourself being tossed around, closed in, or under the rubble already? Or do you see yourself in a fixed position, safe and secure, as a confident observer of the turmoil around you? Restless hearts out of sync with God's heart have developed attachments to unstable things. You're called into a permanent place of rest.

Be aware of the environment you carry within you—the spirit you bring into tumultuous situations. Anchored on the unshakable Rock, see yourself as a carrier of the Kingdom and all its values, attributes, and authority. If the environment inside you is just as stormy as the environment outside you, then you have no authority to speak to the storms. But you are not on your own; the shalom within you comes from God, giving strength to your words and actions. Live as a calmer of storms, an oasis in the desert, an unmovable mountain, having a heart in sync with God's. And be at peace.

PSALM 126: FROM TEARS TO JOY

Those who plant in tears will harvest with shouts of joy.

126:5

When exiles returned to Jerusalem after a long captivity, it was almost too good to be true. They felt like dreamers, laughing and singing songs of joy. The history of God's people is filled with such stories—the exodus from Egypt, the story of redemption, a multitude of personal and communal stories over the course of centuries, and the promise of ultimate triumph over evil—and with songs of victory and gratitude to go with them. God knows how to restore fortunes and make deserts flourish (v. 4), and he knows how to heal our wounded hearts. Sometimes the dreams really do become reality.

So the prayer of verse 4 to restore and renew and the assurances of verses 5-6 that he will reward tearful planters with a joyful harvest are perfectly sensible. Those prayers and assurances may have come in the context described in Haggai 1:2-11, where returnees were told that their harvests were failing because they had not prioritized rebuilding God's house (seeking his presence). But even there they were given the hope of fulfillment. God welcomes our prayers to fill the deserts of our lives with streams, and he promises to replace our tears with joy. This is how his Kingdom works because it reflects the heart of the King.

RE-ENVISION YOUR HARVEST

Whatever has held you captive, whatever reason for the tears that have accompanied the seeds you've sown in the fields, whatever longing or dream seems ever in front of you without coming closer—refuse to see God as the one withholding what you seek. Keep envisioning the redemption and the restoration of your greatest needs and God-given desires. Your tears water the ground where his promises are planted, and one day you'll see a rich harvest from them. And like the returning exiles, you'll be filled with songs of laughter and joy.

Unless the LORD builds a house, the work of the builders is wasted.

127:1

It's only fitting that a psalm about the Lord building a house would be "of Solomon"—whether by him, for him, or in his name. Of all people, he knew the divine help needed to build something as important and sacred as the Temple. It makes sense that returning exiles would embrace that vision as they rebuilt the Temple and Jerusalem. They had a massive task before them, and human hands and ingenuity were not enough.

This psalm is about more than rebuilding a temple and a city, though. It's also about building households and families (vv. 2-5). It's human nature to assume those burdens—to get up early, stay up late, and worry—as if it all depends on how long and hard we work. And while God certainly honors hard work (Proverbs assures us of that), he never tells us to depend on it as the sole formula for success. If *anything* we build is going to bear lasting fruit in the Kingdom, it needs to bear the marks of divine empowerment from beginning to end.

RE-ENVISION YOUR CREATIVITY

God does not send us out into the world to build, create, manage, earn, cultivate, and produce on our own. He invites us into partnership with him. In fact, he is the source of all creativity and strength. He has brilliant ideas. Those who tune in to his voice and give themselves to the flow of his Spirit experience creative breakthroughs, divine solutions, and the energy and vision to persevere.

Refuse to see yourself as the bearer of burdens or the sole source of your own productivity in work, family, or anything else. Envision the divine Partner standing next to you, leading you, filling and energizing you, and blessing the work you and he do together. Your work alone will not last. Yours and his in partnership endures forever and bears everlasting fruit.

PSALM 128: JOYFUL FEAR

How joyful are those who fear the LORD—all who follow his ways!

128:1

The previous psalm casts a vision of work in partnership with God and children as his blessing. That vision expands here, with labor as prosperous and joyful (v. 2), and godly, thriving children as an inheritance (v. 3). To whom are such blessings given? Those who fear the Lord and follow his ways (v. 1).

In many respects, this follows the promise of Psalm 1—that those who delight in God's instruction are like trees planted on the riverbank. In other ways, it extends Aaron's blessing to those who have looked to God as their source of life and peace (Numbers 6:24-26). If we needed a visual of God's face shining upon his people, this is it.

Fearing God is not a popular topic, of course. Perhaps it's a matter of semantics; we use *fear* for so many things, most of them bad. The words *awe* and *respect* capture the idea better, but not completely. We have no perfect words for the overwhelming impulse to change our lives and walk with the renewed vision that comes from encountering God. Many people in Scripture and later history have had life-altering experiences in his presence, and they struggle to describe it. Finite words are never enough for infinite realities.

RE-ENVISION YOUR INSPIRATION

When we read psalms of blessing like this one, our instinct is to do the things (make the changes) they recommend. But even more important is the source that inspires and provokes change. Ask God for life-altering encounters with him. Pray to see things as they are, to have such an enormous vision that it shapes everything about you. See his face shining upon you to fill your life with good things—fruitful labor, abundant blessings, loved ones who love him, a rich and meaningful life, and a lasting inheritance. He delights to give all this to those who delight in him—certainly in the age to come, but even now. It is your calling and privilege to walk in awe and wonder every day.

PSALM 129: UNBOUND

The LORD is good; he has cut me free from the ropes of the ungodly.

129:4

The people of Israel had a history of experiencing oppression—not just once, but on multiple occasions. Egypt, Assyria, Babylon, and a host of minor antagonists enslaved, harassed, or conquered them. Sometimes their suffering was the result of their own rebellion, but that made it no less traumatic. They could easily have been crushed under a sense of inferiority and futility, yet God repeatedly delivered them. He even kept repeating promises of redemption and restoration. It's hard to feel inferior and defeated when the God of the universe is on your side. At some point, you begin to define yourself by his victories instead of your failures and by your future more than your past.

Finding our identity in our past is a temptation for all of us. Most of us have no trouble remembering or even dwelling on our failures. Our wounds and scars are painfully obvious to our own eyes. But when God sets us free from the ropes of evil, we have no reason to continue defining ourselves by our mistakes and sufferings. The God who redeemed us from them has the right to say who we are and how he wants to use us, restore us, and bless us.

RE-ENVISION YOUR FREEDOM

Your vision of yourself and God's vision of you are not the same thing. You may have done well to align your identity with his definition of who you are, but none of us sees ourselves as clearly as he does. Discard the opinions of others and anything in your past that continues to define you, other than his redemptive, restoring work in your life. He has cut the ropes that held you captive. He turns back in shameful defeat anyone or anything that stands in the way of your blessing, just as he did for Jerusalem (v. 5). Let the promise and vision of your future shape you. When God's face shines upon you, no other opinion matters.

I am counting on the LORD. . . . I have put my hope in his word. I long for the Lord more than sentries long for the dawn, yes, more than sentries long for the dawn.

130:5-6

In this psalm of repentance, the psalmist calls out from the depths of despair. The guilt (and likely the consequences) of his sin is a crushing weight; he longs not only for forgiveness but also for freedom and reassurance that he and his people are still in God's graces. It's an appropriate prayer for pilgrims ascending to Jerusalem to confess sins, make sacrifices, and celebrate their redemptive story. The psalmist knows God has promised to forgive, and he craves a renewed fellowship with him. He has fixed his eyes on the Promiser like a watchman waiting for the sun to rise.

That's what eyes of faith do with any of God's promises. It's the posture taken by any believer who hasn't given up through all the trauma and turbulence of life. Our disappointments may fill our vision in long, painful seasons, but at some point we have to shift our gaze to our Redeemer and Restorer. Eagerly, longingly, achingly we watch for the sunrise, the fulfillment of God's promise for a new day.

RE-ENVISION THE WAIT

While you watch, remember to focus not on what hasn't happened yet but on what has been promised. His answer may not fit your expectations or your timing, but it will fit his purposes for you. The gap between promise and fulfillment, regardless of its nature—whether an opportunity to extend forgiveness, call out to him in prayer, restore a broken relationship, or realize a calling—is not a time for despair but for kindling hope and faith. It is an invitation to draw closer to the God you depend on and experience his tenderness and encouragement there. In those moments, his words sink deeper into your heart and thrive there for a lifetime. See the opportunity for what it is, and trust that the dawn will come.

PSALM 131: LIKE A CALMED CHILD

I have calmed and quieted myself. . . . Yes, like a weaned child is my soul within me.

131:2

Zephaniah prophesied Judah's overthrow and captivity, but also its redemption and restoration. In one of the most comforting verses in Scripture, he portrays God as "a mighty savior" yet also tender, like a mother calming her crying infant with her love (Zephaniah 3:17). It's a simultaneously masculine and feminine image, both strong and gentle, in which God promises to fight for and calm his oppressed and frightened people.

This psalm of ascent assumes a similar image in a quiet child calmly trusting his or her Father. The people of Israel were often in an utterly vulnerable position, and though human instinct urges action, the better response was usually patience and rest. The previous psalm urged Israel to hope in the Lord (130:7), and this one presents a picture of what hope looks like, before reiterating the same call to hope in him "now and always" (v. 3). The psalmist sets great and awesome matters aside (v. 1) and determines not to try to figure everything out. Perhaps this is a reminder to the people not to place their hope in a temple or rebuilt city walls rather than in God himself, or maybe it's just general advice for whenever life gets complicated. In any case, it focuses our gaze not on whys and why-nots but on the Lord who holds his children in his arms.

RE-ENVISION YOUR DEFENDER

If you don't see God as your mighty defender, your heart will not rest, and you'll feel compelled to do something—anything—now. The intensity and urgency of our circumstances often speak louder than his reassurances. But if you envision him as your warrior, a Father who is both tender and vigilant in your defense, you can quiet yourself in his love. Let that vision grow. Plenty of distractions will try to bring it back down to just a nice thought rather than a rock-solid promise, but be insistent with the imagery collected in your heart. Wean yourself from reactive impulses, embrace the calming of his words, and rest like a trusting child.

PSALM 132: A KINGDOM OF RESTORATION

Let us go to the sanctuary of the LORD; let us worship at the footstool of his throne.

132:7

Pilgrims to Jerusalem after the Exile and return would have set their sights on the Temple—even if it hadn't been rebuilt yet—and rejoiced at the restoration God was accomplishing. This psalm is a prayer for that restoration to be thoroughly completed. The psalmist longs for a restored dynasty of David (v. 10), which God promises (v. 17). He recounts David's commitment to build a sanctuary for God (vv. 2-5) and recalls God's vow to David to establish his throne forever (vv. 11-12). The language points in places to both the installation of the Ark in Jerusalem (1 Chronicles 15–16) and Solomon's prayer of dedication for the Temple (2 Chronicles 6–7), both of which were landmark events in Israel's history, establishing the city and Temple as God's "footstool" (Psalm 132:7), his dwelling place amid his people. The entire psalm emphasizes this connection between God and Jerusalem's Temple, and the vows on both sides that established it. The psalmist pleads for recapturing what seems to have been lost.

For centuries, the church has majored on the gospel of redemption but not fully explored the gospel of restoration, other than to cast it into a future age when Jesus comes again. But what is the growth of the Kingdom about, here and now, if not restoration? If the Kingdom promise involves a "final restoration of all things" (Acts 3:21), Kingdom expansion in this age will surely involve some degree of restoration too.

RE-ENVISION RESTORATION

The gospel of the Kingdom includes spiritual salvation, but there's a greater fullness to the message. God doesn't promise just to take everyone to heaven; he promises a new heaven and a new earth, full of resurrected bodies. We are not just being saved from the penalty of sin but being restored from its ravages. This is his ministry to us personally, but he also calls us to be agents of restoration in the world. He is on a mission to make all things new. As his new creations, this is our mission too.

PSALM 133: A GOOD AND PLEASANT GIFT

How wonderful and pleasant it is when brothers live together in harmony!

133:1

To us, the oil of Aaron (v. 2) and the dew of Mount Hermon (v. 3) are obscure terms, but to ancient Israelite readers, they were loaded with meaning. Aaron was anointed with oil as the father of Israel's priests, his head and beard thoroughly covered in order to sanction him, set him apart, and signify his empowerment by the Spirit for his priestly role. As a priest, he would represent humanity to God and God to humanity, especially in the context of prayer and worship together. The connection between God and his people flowed freely, just like the oil poured over a priest's head.

Mount Hermon, ancient Israel's highest peak, stood at its northern border, its dew and snowmelt making the land green and fruitful. The idea of its dew falling on Mount Zion instead was a beautiful dream that would have made the holy city perpetually fruitful and its people perpetually blessed. These images depicted the restored Israel as overflowing with God's goodness.

At the center of this picture is unity—the fellowship of God's people living in harmony with each other. In a fractured, fragmented world (and church), we might see this unity as an unreachable utopian ideal. Yet unity both reflects and invites God's presence and makes our fellowship fruitful. In God's eyes, it is a good and pleasant gift.

RE-ENVISION UNITY

In our individualist age, we tend to see our faith as a personal gift we can share with others when we gather. God sees it as a corporate gift we can take with us when we're alone. Our fellowship is not a casual matter to him; it's where spiritual gifts are imparted and exercised, his Word and his voice are shared with the body of believers, and our fellowship is enlivened by his Spirit. He loves our alone time with him, but he especially inhabits the gathering. Learn to see it as central to your faith. Seek harmony with other believers. And like God, enjoy how wonderful and pleasant it is.

PSALM 134: AGENTS OF BLESSING

May the LORD, who made heaven and earth, bless you from Jerusalem.

134:3

In this last of the Psalms of Ascent, departing pilgrims leave with an image of worship leaders and Temple workers exalting God in this place of his presence. On behalf of the community, the psalmist blesses the entire Temple apparatus—priests, Levites, musicians, caretakers, and more—but also, by implication, all of God's people. The words of Aaron's blessing have appeared throughout the Psalms of Ascent, and one last word here represents that blessing as a whole.

The background image is not just Mount Zion; it's God in the midst of his people everywhere, whether they are in Jerusalem to worship and participate in Israel's feasts or returning to their home, wherever that happens to be. God is still among them. They know he is being worshiped night and day at the Temple, and they also know they can worship him anywhere. His connection with his people, no matter how far it is stretched, is just as alive and full of energy as if they were right there in the Temple courts.

RE-ENVISION THE BLESSING

See yourself as an agent of blessing. God gave Aaron's blessing to Israel's priests so they could declare it over the people throughout the ages (Numbers

6:22-27). As priests—every believer is one, after all (1 Peter 2:5, 9; Revelation 1:6; 5:10)—our words carry power to impart God's blessing to each other. We are commanded to bless others, even those who make themselves our enemies (Matthew 5:44; Romans 12:14). In fact, when we look around at a world that seems to be missing out on God's blessing and feel a spiritual impulse to do something about it, we need to remember that *we have the power to bless*. We should be using it liberally.

Envision yourself as an agent of blessing, a fountain of words that declare life, build people up, and impart shalom as far and wide as you can—to family members, friends, acquaintances, and even those hostile to your faith. God wants to pour out his mercy on this world. Our words are one of his primary means for doing so.

PSALM 135: ABOVE ALL GODS

The LORD does whatever pleases him throughout all heaven and earth.

135:6

Echoing the words of Psalm 115:4-8, this psalm denounces idolatry, pointing out the impotence of false gods and how those who make idols become like them. In contrast, the God of Israel is so powerful that he can do whatever he pleases. He presides over forces of nature—genuinely, unlike local storm gods. He delivered his people from Egypt by sending plagues upon their captors and gave them the land he promised, in spite of all the hostile inhabitants there. For that and many other reasons, he should be praised—a refrain that permeates this psalm from beginning to end. He is clearly greater (and truer) than all the other gods out there.

The Egyptian Hallel (Psalms 113–118) celebrated the exodus from Egypt. The Psalms of Ascent (Psalms 120–134) celebrated the exodus from Babylonian/Persian captivity. This psalm and the next return to the flight from Egypt but were written after the Captivity. In sum, they rejoice in God's sovereignty over history and his ultimate purposes for his people. At the time, those purposes seemed to be the restoration of Zion. As we now know—and as Hebrew prophets foretold—his ultimate purposes were global and even cosmic, a display of his glorious nature for all heaven and earth to behold.

RE-ENVISION YOUR VINDICATION

Many in the world still look down on those who believe. They think we're naive, foolish, or judgmental haters. Oblivious to how real and good God is, they often talk about him as our imaginary friend or oppressive master. Meanwhile, their gods are impotent to save them from their own impulses, depression, anxiety, moral consequences, and self-destructive behaviors.

The promise of this psalm and of all Scripture is that God will vindicate his people—often in the here and now, certainly in the there and then. We "naive fools" who believe in him will prove incredibly wise in time. Living with that assurance today eliminates our knee-jerk reactions and vigorous defenses. Like Jesus, we can endure insults and not be offended, seeing our accusers as wounded souls in need of a loving Savior.

His faithful love endures forever.

136:1-26

At the dedication of Solomon's Temple, when fire came down and God's glorious presence filled the place, the people fell face down, declared God's goodness, and shouted, "His faithful love endures forever!" (2 Chronicles 7:3). This psalm repeats that phrase again and again, presumably as a refrain shouted by the congregation in a Temple worship service. It has become the "Great Hallel," a celebration used in the morning service of Sabbaths and feasts, often paired with the previous psalm and in some respects related to the Egyptian Hallel (Psalms 113–118). And there's no mistaking its focus: God's *hesed*, a Hebrew term denoting his faithful, enduring love, kindness, and favor.

The psalm recites many of God's great works in creation and on behalf of Israel—all of them miraculous and all reflections of his compassion. Even his works of judgment are motivated by love. The New Testament emphasizes his love throughout: God so loved the world that he sent Jesus (John 3:16); we need the Holy Spirit's power to even comprehend the width, length, height, and depth of God's love (Ephesians 3:16-19); and love is God's defining characteristic (1 John 4:8, 16). Anyone who wants to know him needs to begin with this foundation.

RE-ENVISION HIS LOVE

The problem is that many of us have treated his love as *only* foundational—the most basic truth of Christianity that even kids in Sunday school have learned. We've seen it as an elemental truth, something to grow beyond as we explore the mysteries of God's nature and apply his truth to the complex issues of our world. We long for something deeper.

There is nothing deeper. We need to be captivated once again by a vision of God's love—how it is the driving force, the core energy, the supernatural center of the universe that, if we dive into it fully, empowers us to do his works. We cannot move beyond this, only away from it or into it further. Immersed in his faithfulness, saturated in his kindness, bathed in the light of his love, we become like him and live in the power that created the world itself.

How can we sing the songs of the LORD while in a pagan land?

137:4

Life in Babylonian captivity was difficult for Judah's faithful. The Temple was rubble, so no sacrifices were being performed on behalf of the nation and no feasts could be celebrated in Jerusalem. The foreign customs were unfamiliar and often offensive. The food was not kosher. The names they were given invoked Babylon's false gods. And some of their people's leaders, including priests, were being "re-educated" to integrate into Babylonian society. It was virtually impossible to follow the laws of Moses or live a thoroughly biblical lifestyle. They were far from home in more ways than one.

Many of us face similar problems in our world today. We don't have the same concerns about dietary restrictions or distinctive dress, and our culture can be pretty accommodating on many points. But it has altered how we live out the biblical concepts of community, complicated our moral understanding, and hindered any efforts at a lifestyle of biblical simplicity. In many ways, like scattered Jews, we've adapted our values to our surroundings while trying to keep our distinctions the best we can. Unlike the psalmist, we don't resort to curses or the violent emotions that provoke them (vv. 7-9)—Scripture often acknowledges honest reactions without endorsing them. But we do sing the Lord's songs in a world that dances to very different tunes.

RE-ENVISION YOUR DISTINCTIVENESS

God has not called us to legalism, and to some degree he wants us to integrate with the rest of society. We live in this world, even if we aren't of it. But we do need to see ourselves as foreigners (John 17:14-16; Philippians 3:20; Hebrews 11:13; 1 Peter 2:11), aliens in another land, ambassadors representing a homeland that is not very far away but still quite different from where we are. While many Christians try to minimize their differences to avoid standing out, God often uses these differences to show the world a better way. As travelers passing through a foreign landscape, we set our hearts on a much truer realm and sing the Lord's songs with joy.

PSALM 138: A CERTAIN PURPOSE

The LORD will fulfill his purpose for me. . . . Do not forsake the work of your hands.

138:8, ESV

The last collection of Davidic psalms (Psalms 138–145) repositions Israel's worship in Jerusalem. It's a fitting approach to the end of the book, geographically coming full circle, chronologically rooting Israel's praise in the life of the king who so zealously established the city as a worship center, and redemptively declaring the reestablishment of the dynasty that was prophesied to last forever. It's especially gratifying in its placement right after the most plaintive song of the Exile (Psalm 137). And it begins here with wholehearted worship (138:1). Later it includes a prophecy that all the kings of earth will sing songs of Zion that exiles in the previous psalm strained to sing (vv. 4-5). Finally, it expresses confidence that the Lord will fulfill his purposes for the psalmist (v. 8)—a reasonable trust, since he was fulfilling them for the nation too.

Yet in spite of this confidence, the voice of David asks God not to forsake or abandon his work. The work is promised but not yet complete. It doesn't just happen by fate—the prayers of God's people and his faithful love (v. 8) will ensure it. In the partnership between God and his people, God will surely answer this request to fulfill his purposes.

RE-ENVISION YOUR FUTURE

Paul would answer this plea with a promise: "He who has begun a good work in you will complete it until the day of Jesus Christ" (Philippians 1:6, NKJV). You may envision your future as up in the air; even God's purposes for you might not feel secure. But God doesn't start projects without intending to finish them. He has the foresight to know how things will turn out; he knows what will advance his purposes and benefit his people. The fact that he began his work in you—and for you and through you—points to a glorious end. Whatever he has promised you, whatever gifts he has given you, whatever calling he has placed in your heart, he will not forsake it. It will find fulfillment somehow, somewhere, sometime.

Search me, O God, and know my heart; test me and know my anxious thoughts. Point out anything in me that offends you, and lead me along the path of everlasting life.

139:23-24

For a people long trapped in exile, these words written by (or in honor of) David would be profoundly comforting. Yes, it was hard to sing the songs of Zion in a foreign land of pagan gods (137:4). But the God of Zion was right there with them, just as he had been with David in every moment of his long years of exile from Saul. As the psalmist reassures, our entire lives, including our innermost thoughts, are open books in God's presence (139:1-4). Even when our past seems obscure and our future seems uncertain, he is already intimately acquainted with both.

In a world full of localized, national gods, Israel's God was radically unique—omnipresent, omniscient, and omnipotent. But such terms hardly capture the intimacy of the God who knows every fiber of our being, every thought in our minds, and every detail of our coming days. Such knowledge is frightening through the lens of our insecurities but supremely comforting in our darkest moments. If we had any reservations about surrendering to this God, any fear he might try to force us into a plan that doesn't fit us, any suspicion that he doesn't have our best interests in mind, his loving care from day one ought to relieve us (vv. 15-16). He knows us better than we know ourselves.

RE-ENVISION YOUR THOUGHT LIFE

Like the psalmist, we have "anxious thoughts." We might see them for what they say about ourselves, but God may see them for what they say about him—our fears that he might not guard our future, walk with us through troubled times, be able to calm our fears, or provide for us in times of need. In effect, they are the opposite of worship, statements against his loving care. No wonder the psalmist is concerned about rooting out offensive thoughts (vv. 23-24). The path of everlasting life is filled with worship and trust, as we offer praises to the God who created us, knows everything about us, and invites us into the deepest intimacy we can ever know.

LORD, do not let evil people have their way. Do not let their evil schemes succeed.

140:8

Most of us will never encounter the physical dangers faced by David, by Israel's unpopular prophets, by the captive Jews, or by the former exiles seeking to rebuild Jerusalem (as in Nehemiah 4). We do, however, walk through a world of enormous spiritual dangers. Our spiritual enemies aim to deceive, distract, demean, discourage, damage, and demolish. Or, as Jesus put it, the thief comes "to steal and kill and destroy" (John 10:10). Even for the Israelites rebuilding their city, who faced the dangers of physical threats or psychological warfare from external enemies, along with the emotional stresses of internal strife, the stakes were almost always higher than they appeared on the surface.

That's still true for all of God's people. The manifestations of the spiritual battle are many. When we pray for God's Kingdom to come (Matthew 6:10), we're also praying for another kingdom to go, and there will always be opposition in this age. Through the emotional wounds and distorted intellects of human beings separated from God, the enemy casts accusations and raises up opposition to our callings and to the advancement of God's Kingdom. Our journey in life takes us through a minefield of evil devices and dangerous traps (vv. 4-5).

RE-ENVISION THE THREATS

All those realities might tempt us to react with fear or even panic, but only if we give them power they don't actually have. In reality, as this psalm and others assure us, God protects and rescues us, even when we aren't fully aware of the dangers. We get to pull up a chair and watch God work in these strange, tumultuous times. If your natural eyes are glued to visual evidence, you might get very discouraged. But if your spiritual eyes can discern how God is setting things up for great deliverances, awakenings, and unveilings, you might get excited. Those who trust him to thwart evil and accomplish great things will find their trust rewarded.

PSALM 141: A SWEET AROMA

Accept my prayer as incense offered to you, and my upraised hands as an evening offering.

141:2

Opposition in the previous psalm came in the form of a frontal attack. In this one, it comes as a subtle influence. The psalmist prays not to drift into evil (v. 4) and asks for correction (v. 5). He senses the traps around him and desperately wants to resist the seduction of an ungodly environment. So he prays constantly—for himself (vv. 1, 8) and against the wicked (v. 5)—and he trusts that his prayers will rise to God like the incense of a sacrifice (v. 2).

Incense represented God's presence and was offered morning and evening at the Temple. It was a costly offering that produced a sweet but strong aroma. Only priests were allowed to offer it on the altar, but there were no prohibitions against seeing it as a symbol of prayer. And it symbolized prayer beautifully—continually rising to heaven, pleasing to God, and lingering in its effects. Like incense, heartfelt, passionate prayer fills the air with a beautiful scent.

A lifestyle of prayer continually invites God's intervention and manifest presence into the circumstances of our lives. Whether we need safeguards like the psalmist, or we need provision, opportunities, or any other blessing from heaven, prayer is meant to be much more than making a request. It fills the air of our lives with the connection between heaven and earth.

RE-ENVISION YOUR PRAYERS

Imagine being in God's throne room, where worshiping, attending angels bring the fragrant incense of human prayers into his presence (Revelation 5:8; 8:3-5). It's a beautiful scene. There are no shot-in-the-dark prayers here, only the precious requests of God's people who believe in and depend on his wisdom, power, and love. What loving father would ignore such pleas from his children? Not this one. They are heartfelt statements of trust in his goodness.

Envision your prayers as that kind of offering. Make them a lifestyle that fills the air of heaven with faith. You may not enjoy the process between prayer and answer, but God enjoys what comes from it. He is always pleased with the aroma rising from your heart to his.

PSALM 142: GOD IS YOUR PORTION

You are my refuge, my portion in the land of the living.

142:5, NKJV

During one season of his flight from Saul, David hid in the cave of Adullam (1 Samuel 22:1-2). It became his refuge, his fortress, even his rallying point, as many allies joined him there. Many would see the cave as David's help, but David had learned to see God alone as his help. When he was overwhelmed, God would know which way he should turn (Psalm 142:3).

No matter how desperate a situation looks to us, God is never in a desperate situation. Neither are those who trust in him for answers. When we're hemmed in, God knows the way out. When we're lost, he knows how to get us wherever we're going. When we're surrounded with threats, he surrounds us with protection. The more we become convinced of his help, the more our sense of being overwhelmed dissipates.

That's why this psalmist expresses confidence that God will "deal bountifully" with him (v. 7, NKJV), and why he declares that God is his "portion" (v. 5, NKJV). Israel's priests did not receive a tract of land to make their living like non-Levitical tribes did, because God said he himself would be their allotment (Numbers 18:20). Some might have been disappointed about having no piece of the Promised Land as an inheritance, but they got something much better: the Promiser.

RE-ENVISION YOUR ALLOTMENT

Embracing God as your "portion" echoes the thought of another psalmist—"Whom have I in heaven but you? I desire you more than anything on earth" (73:25). It's a captivating vision, isn't it? Which is better: to own a piece of land or be an heir of the God who owns the entire earth? If you have a limited inheritance, you only get that inheritance. But if you're in Christ, filled with the Spirit of God, you have every spiritual blessing and all his resources too. Having God as your portion, your inheritance, is comprehensively fulfilling. Whether you're in a mansion or a cave, what else could you ever need?

PSALM 143: UNFAILING LOVE

Let me hear of your unfailing love each morning, for I am trusting you. Show me where to walk, for I give myself to you.

143:8

This last penitential psalm is not as introspective or desperate as the others. The psalmist sees himself as a sinner, and he is aware that "no one is innocent" before God (v. 2)—a thought emphasized by New Testament writers, particularly Paul, in teaching that we are justified by grace through faith alone (Ephesians 2:8-9). Even so, the psalmist is repentant. Yet he is also full of urgent requests. As in the previous psalm, he is "paralyzed with fear" (v. 4).

One way to get beyond that overwhelming feeling is to remember all the great things God has done in days of old (v. 5). When we recall his works and his ways in the lives of biblical and historical characters and in our own experience, we see a pattern—a God who meets us in our brokenness, not just telling us the truth about it but walking us through it and healing us from it. He enters our desperation, pain, and losses, offering his power, restoration, and inheritance, and we come out victorious, healed, and whole. He pours himself out for us, in us, and through us.

RE-ENVISION HIS LOVE

As recipients of his unfailing love (v. 8), we also enter people's brokenness and lead them out into wholeness. Or, as John once put it, "we love because he first loved us" (1 John 4:19, ESV). We can't do that without a revelation of God's love in the first place, which is why Paul prayed for believers to be supernaturally empowered to grasp all the dimensions of the love of Christ (Ephesians 3:16-19). A vision of the intimate love of our Father flowing constantly into our lives unravels anxiety, defuses fears, and frees us from the sense of oppression the psalmist feels here. It also makes us patient in times of trouble. We have no need for panic; we know our Father will come through.

Praise the LORD, who is my rock. He trains my hands for war and gives my fingers skill for battle.

144:1

In the spirit of Psalm 18, this royal psalm celebrates David's victories and prays for more. The psalmist praises God's nature as our loving ally, fortress, tower of safety, rescuer, and shield (v. 2). He asks God to open the heavens and come down (v. 5). And he pronounces a series of benedictions (vv. 12-14) that envision the shalom of God's Kingdom, affirm the return of covenant blessings in place of curses (per Deuteronomy 28), and reflect the messianic age. It's a comforting, hopeful, even empowering message, not only in David's time but also in the age of restoration after Israel's exile—and in our time today.

The previous psalm concluded the Psalter's laments and complaints. We are left now with praise and celebration—still with some requests, though in a hopeful tone; and still with some enemies present, though also with the clear expectation of defeating them. Amid all the celebrations, statements of faith and dependence are clear. These victories don't really belong to Israel or its kings. They belong to God.

Scripture gives us two approaches to battle, and we have to embrace them both. On the one hand, the battle belongs to the Lord (Exodus 14:13-14; 2 Chronicles 20:15, 17). On the other hand, he trains our hands and sends us out to fight (Psalm 144:1). Strength and victory are in his hands; going out to the battlefield, even if only to be there as his vessels, is in ours. He does it all, but he usually does it through his people.

RE-ENVISION YOUR BATTLES

Learn to see God not only as your helper in battle but also as the one who fights for you. See your faith as the means to put the victory in his hands (2 Chronicles 20:20), your worship as the environment he inhabits (2 Chronicles 20:21-22; Psalm 22:3), and his Word as the sword that cuts through enemy schemes (2 Corinthians 10:4; Ephesians 6:17). He will certainly defeat the enemies of your soul for you. But be ready: He will also defeat them *through* you.

You open your hand and satisfy the desires of every living thing.

145:16, NIV

In the spirit of Psalm 103, in which David told his soul to bless the Lord, this psalm asserts his will to exalt God (v. 1), praise him every day and forever (vv. 1-2, 21), meditate on his splendor and miracles (v. 5), and proclaim his greatness (v. 6). He also declares similar praise from others (vv. 7, 10-12). But mostly he points to the glories of God and his reign. This last of the Davidic psalms focuses on God's Kingdom and the ideal society it engenders. Even more importantly, it focuses on the King and what he is like.

Throughout this hymn of praise, the theme of God's generosity comes through. He is good to everyone (v. 9), keeps his promises (v. 13), helps the fallen (v. 14), satisfies the desires of all his creatures (v. 16), is close to those who call on him (v. 18), and rescues and fulfills those who fear him (v. 19). There is no hard master or stern commander in this psalm. It is clear that God wants us to be satisfied with life—not selfishly or superficially so, but with the fullness of joy he offers.

RE-ENVISION YOUR DESIRES

If you've ever seen your desires as hindrances to your discipleship, reconsider where they come from and what they mean. Envision them as an important point of connection with God. Some of them may not fit his purposes for you, but many of them have been put into your heart by his own design. They are a stage for him to display his goodness. He is honored when we are fulfilled—when he fulfills desires, we are satisfied with how he fulfills them and can enjoy his gifts fully. This is a testimony to his nature. There's no need for self-deprivation born of the assumption that he is hesitant to be generous with us. Enjoy his abundance in whatever form it comes, be grateful for it, and show the world how good your Father is.

Joyful are those who have the God of Israel as their helper, whose hope is in the Lord their God.

146:5

God is good all the time. Our theology raises no objections to that statement; but our hearts might, especially during a dark and difficult season. Israel and its psalmists went through all sorts of dark and difficult seasons, even from the start. The patriarchal history is full of dysfunction and pain. The entire clan that grew into a nation was captive in Egypt for centuries. Their escape and wilderness wanderings were traumatic and long. Their victories in the Promised Land were significant but incomplete. Their cycle of rebellion, repentance, and restoration resulted in repeated oppression. Their first experiments with kingship failed. Their split after Solomon's reign led to centuries of corruption and idolatry. Their defeat by Assyria and captivity in Babylon were catastrophic existential crises. And their efforts to rebuild Jerusalem and its Temple were vigorously contested every step of the way. Yet God was good all the time.

Many of the psalms, even those that begin in crisis, are filled with joy. The Psalter itself ends with a string of psalms that are nothing but praise. These are the songs of a people who have learned that—with the God above all gods on their side—all things are available, possible, doable, and believable. And for that, they could celebrate with deep-down, lasting joy.

RE-ENVISION YOUR JOY

Joy is a blessing not only to those who have it. It's one of the greatest gifts you can give to the people around you, as well as the greatest testimony you can give to the world. It's especially powerful when you've gone through trials and pain. When your life overflows with the joy of the Kingdom, you become a display of the Kingdom's true nature. People see what God is like in you. Picture your fullness of joy not only as a comfort to your soul but also as a blessing to the world. Rivers of life flow through it into thirsty hearts around you.

Sing out your thanks to the LORD. . . . The LORD's delight is in those who fear him, those who put their hope in his unfailing love.

147:7, 11

God gave his creatures natural strength for a reason. We couldn't function without it. And as impressively as humanity has stretched its physical potential—athletic and military prowess keep increasing, and records keep being broken—God takes no pleasure in people relying on their own abilities (v. 10). He delights in those who put their hopes entirely in his power. We were designed to depend fully on him.

And why wouldn't we? This and the previous two psalms (and many others) have lavished praise on him for all the wonderful things he does. No problem is beyond his power to solve, no sin beyond his mercy to forgive, no person too lost and broken for him to rescue and heal. Given a choice between our power and his, we'd be fools to opt for ours. His many blessings and benefits are available by faith. According to the practice of many psalmists, including this one, we can even go ahead and thank him for them.

RE-ENVISION YOUR GRATITUDE

Most people think that gratitude comes after God's gifts and that truly grateful people are those who have been given a lot. But in God's Kingdom, gratitude comes before the gift (as well as after). A bitter heart never leads to a full and abundant life, but a thankful heart does. God seems to often respond to our gratitude even more readily than he responds to our prayer requests.

We see this pattern in the Psalms—people in crisis crying out to God but also thanking him before the answer comes. Paul likewise urged the Philippians to petition God with thanksgiving in their hearts, not just for what he had already done but also for what he was going to do in response to their requests (Philippians 4:6). Value your thankfulness not only for the appreciation it expresses but also for the environment it creates. God steps into that environment with all his generous goodness.

PSALM 148: VOICES OF PRAISE

Let every created thing give praise to the LORD, for he issued his command, and they came into being.

148:5

God is worthy of praise. This psalm calls for praise to come from every direction—from the skies above and the land and seas below, from planets and stars, from angelic and human beings and the animal kingdom, from kings and everyone under them, young and old alike. It's a declaration of his glory, but it goes deeper than a theological statement. It's filled with admiration, even love. It's a prayer of worship and adoration.

Praise and adoration are normal human responses to God's transcendence and majesty, but they are often lacking in our prayers. We come to God with long lists of needs, pains, problems, and grievances. That's natural too; we know how desperate and dependent we are. But behind the requests is an assumption of our relationship with him, and that relationship is designed to be based on and filled with love. So are our conversations.

Something happens when we focus on adoring God. We are immersed in the climate of his Kingdom and the atmosphere of his throne room, where revelations of his nature are far more easily seen than anywhere else. Adoration brings his attributes to life in our minds, hearts, and circumstances; thoroughly changes the tone of our prayers; and sparks breakthroughs in situations that have seemed unmovable, oppressive, complicated, and destructive. It brings heaven into our souls.

RE-ENVISION YOUR ADORATION

See your prayers as environment-shifters and fill them with adoration. Yes, they are conversations with God, but we've all experienced the power of conversations to lift us up, bring us down, or take us places we've never been. They can fill a room with laughter and joy, cultivate a sense of intimacy, and bring us closer to those we love. Requests alone don't do that; expressions of affection do. Fill your prayers with praise and adoration, let them set the tone of your life, and invite God's manifest presence into it.

Sing to the LORD a new song. . . . Praise his name with dancing, accompanied by tambourine and harp.

149:1, 3

The Kingdom of God is a celebration. Yes, there is work to be done and people to bring in, but what are we bringing them in to? If it isn't a huge celebration, something is missing. The Psalms repeatedly tell us to be filled with joy, worship the Lord, shout our praises, tell of his goodness, and exult in his name. They also tell us to sing and dance. Like the father of the prodigal, our Father enjoys a good celebration (Luke 15:7, 22-23), and his Son really knows how to liven up a party (John 2:1-10). As serious as life can be, we can't forget that we are headed toward an exuberant, extravagant wedding feast.

Some people might call our singing and dancing, whatever form they take, "living in denial." Others might think it's undignified (see 2 Samuel 6:16, 21-22). Yet God persistently called Israel to rejoice in him, even in times of battle and captivity, and to keep rejoicing regardless of how it made them appear to more "sensible" people. That doesn't mean there's no place for grief and sorrow—the Bible is also full of appropriate laments—but among the overarching themes of Scripture are God's matchless worth, our eternal redemption and restoration, and ultimate victory over all that is wrong. Those are worth singing and dancing about!

RE-ENVISION THE THEMES OF YOUR HEART

Perhaps you can think of many reasons not to fill your life with songs and dancing right now. The trials you're experiencing may seem overwhelming, but they all pale in comparison to the big-picture reasons for celebration. Turn your gaze to those larger reasons. Let yourself be preoccupied with the glory of God, the vastness and majesty of his creation, the promises he has made and the victories he has won, the beauty of his plan, and the people he fills with his presence. When your vision is filled with him, your problems appear small and your future bright. And your heart begins to sing and dance.

Let everything that breathes sing praises to the LORD! Praise the LORD!

150:6

The last word in the Psalms is *hallelujah*—meaning literally, "praise the Lord." It doesn't appear in Scripture as often as we might think, and not until the last three psalms of Book 4 (104–106). But it comes up increasingly often from there on, reaching a crescendo as the Psalter closes, as if all creation is awakening to the indescribable glory of the God behind and beyond this universe. As previously mentioned (see "Hallelujah Psalms" on page 238), this term combines the Hebrew words for praise (*halelu*) and Yahweh (*yah*, a shortened form of the name). It became integral to Israel's Temple liturgy and corporate praises. Fittingly, it has transcended Hebrew and is now declared by worshipers in a multitude of languages around the world.

From a heavenly perspective, we can see how worship is the driving force of the universe. What once might have seemed like a boring ritual or an irrelevant distraction now seems central to everything. If we were really created to glorify God and enjoy him forever, as the famous catechism says, "hallelujah" is at the heart of our purpose as human beings. On any given day, there is no higher goal than to be filled with worshipful, grateful, deeply intimate love for God (Matthew 22:36-38). If that doesn't become our lifestyle, then no matter how much we accomplish in life or whose lives we influence, we've fallen short of our purpose.

RE-ENVISION HOW THE UNIVERSE WORKS

God created the universe, and it (and everything in it) revolves around him. From ground level in the midst of a rebellious world, things might appear random or inglorious, or even centered on ourselves. But that's an illusion. When he opens our eyes to see the truth, our hearts are filled with worship, and we are brought back into alignment with the fundamental purpose of creation. That's what's at stake in our worship—the complete reordering of our lives. It's our highest purpose and greatest privilege, to our enormous benefit and God's unfathomable glory, forever.

CONCLUSION

In reading the Psalms and this commentary, perhaps you've felt all the highs and lows and twists and turns as though you've been riding a roller coaster—from overwhelming grief to overwhelming joy, from utter confusion to crystal clear vision, from the agony of defeat to the thrill of victory. The psalmists have taken us through a wide and varied range of human experience.

That's by design. No psalmist planned it this way, but the Spirit who inspired these words has made it clear that he is relevant to everything we go through. God not only inhabits every corner of this universe; he wants to inhabit every corner of our hearts. And in every possible situation we could go through, he wants to be the object of our worship and love.

Perhaps you've thought of worship only as a spiritual high, but as the Psalms show us, it's an appropriate choice in any moment and can express the leaning of our heart in various circumstances. Sometimes the choice to turn our eyes toward God in our darkest moments, however feebly, is high praise indeed. Sometimes calming our hearts and going back to sleep during an anxious night is an act of deep and honoring trust. The resolve to stand firm in our faith even when we're afraid is a statement of worship, even when it doesn't feel like one. The writer of Hebrews would call each of these a "sacrifice of praise" (Hebrews 13:15). These may not be exhilarating in the moment, but they say volumes about our view of God.

If you've ever wondered how to get from point A to point B in your heart—from turmoil to peace, doubt to faith, fear to confidence, despair to hope, or apathy to praise—this is your field manual. Psalms that begin in crisis usually end in resolution, not necessarily in outward events but in inner attitude. We are blessed to have this record of God's people wrestling with circumstances, enemies, themselves, and even God himself in light of his revealed truth.

Let their spiritual journeys shape yours. Expand your vision of worship to encompass every area of your life—every stream of thought, every choice in the heat of battle, every statement of faith in your deepest grief, even every doubt that takes God and truth seriously, and yes, every joyful hallelujah at the altar. A life engaged with God, oriented toward his purposes, and open to his fullness is the heart of worship. And through the Psalms, we learn to worship from the heart.

Acknowledgments

Tracing one's own knowledge to its original sources can be a nearly impossible task. I'm extremely grateful to have benefited from numerous sermons, lectures, commentaries, articles, essays, study materials, and personal conversations over the years, yet I can hardly remember any of them specifically. Our minds often work that way; they assimilate the information we receive and internalize it as "general understanding," as if we came into it ourselves, even when we know we didn't. So it is with my familiarity with the Psalms. I owe a debt to many influences I wish I remembered well enough to thank.

But I can at least acknowledge those whose works I consulted in preparation for writing this devotional commentary, including Walter Brueggemann, C. Hassell Bullock, C. S. Lewis, Tremper Longman, O. Palmer Robertson, Patrick Henry Reardon, Michael Wilcock, Gerald H. Wilson, and the unnamed scholars behind many reference notes. To these and many others, thank you for sharing your insights and expertise.

I am also grateful to the editorial team at Tyndale House Publishers, especially Jon Bryant for his careful and insightful work on this manuscript, as well as my agent, Mark Sweeney, for his encouragement and ever-reliable advice.

And, of course, I will forever be thankful for my wife, Hannah, and the rest of my family for their thoughtful questions, stimulating conversation, comic relief, enduring patience, and unwavering support.

May God fill the lives of all with blessing upon blessing.

Discussion Guide

This devotional commentary works well for individual use, but studying Scripture with other people and discussing biblical truths and insights is a great way to wrestle with and reinforce what you're learning. The following discussion prompts are organized into six manageable, thematic groupings to help get that conversation started. Feel free to condense these groupings into fewer sessions, divide them into more, or adapt them as you wish, depending on your needs and schedule. Do not feel compelled to discuss every question in every section. These are simply suggestions for touching on some of the most important themes of the book.

SESSION 1: INTRODUCTION

1. What parallels do you see, if any, between the polytheistic, idolatrous world inhabited by ancient Israel and our world today? What false "gods" today are competing for the devotion of human hearts? What challenges do we face in making God preeminent in our hearts and minds?

2. Why do you think the Psalms portray God with so many different images? How do these images—for example, Rock, Shepherd, Warrior, King, Fortress—address the many different needs we experience?

3. Some psalms indicate the context in which they were written, and others do not. What are some of the benefits of knowing a psalm's context? What are some of the benefits of not knowing?

4. Taken as a whole, the book of Psalms shows us how to acknowledge and experience God's presence in every area of our lives. Are there any areas of your life that you tend to compartmentalize in order to keep God at a distance? If so, what can you do to overcome this tendency?

5. In what ways do the Psalms demonstrate how we can pour out our hearts to God? How do they show us what kinds of responses we can get from him when we do?

SESSION 2: BOOK 1, PSALMS 1–41

1. In a world of diverse beliefs and practices, the psalmists had to make choices about which king and kingdom they would honor and which source of help they would depend on. What does that look like in our world today? In what ways are we daily presented with the same kinds of choices?

2. Psalm 1 pictures the faithful as flourishing trees shaped by a godly environment. What implications does that image have for the spiritual environment you choose for yourself? Are there any adjustments you need to make to surround yourself with the right influences?

3. Psalm 12 expresses alarm that society is growing worse and more ungodly. Do you hear similar concerns today? Where does that message come from? Why might eyes of faith see that perspective as the wrong focus or even as misguided? In what ways is God's Kingdom expanding?

4. As demonstrated in Psalm 13, why is it important to recognize where you are in the storyline of your life? How does knowing the trajectory of God's plans help you maintain hope?

5. In what ways is God "enthroned" on the praises of his people, as Psalm 22:3 says? How do we invite the power of his presence into situations that need his intervention and influence?

6. How does Psalm 23 reorient our vision of God from seeing him as someone from whom we beg for help to seeing him as someone who actively pursues our welfare? How does this change the way we approach life?

7. In what ways can your problems and pain serve as platforms for God to reveal something about himself, as Psalm 28 shows? If you became more aware of this, how might it change the way you pray when you're in a crisis?

8. In what ways is the invitation to "taste and see" (Psalm 34:8) an invitation to re-envision who God is and what he does? What does it mean to taste and see that God is good? How does he reveal himself to those who seek him?

SESSION 3: BOOK 2, PSALMS 42–72

1. Many of the psalms in Book 2 are testimonies to how we can reorient our vision—away from crises and complications and toward simple faith and trust in God. Why is perspective so important in Scripture? To what degree does it shape our lives? How does the global focus of many psalms in this book help us shift our perspective to greater purposes?

2. In what ways do trust and apathy look similar to outward observers? How does Psalm 46 aim to lift us above the fray of tumultuous, frightening situations?

3. How is thankfulness a sacrifice to God (Psalm 50:14)? Under what circumstances are gratitude, praise, and devotion costly? What do these attitudes say about how we view God?

4. How does Psalm 51 help us no longer view sin and its consequences as irreversible setbacks? How does God help us live with a heart uncluttered by sin, guilt, and shame?

5. Who do you see as the carrier of your burdens—yourself, the people around you, or God? What does Psalm 55 urge us to do with our burdens? What is God's response when we give them to him?

6. What attitudes and expressions does Psalm 66 urge us to focus on in a world that needs to know God? What are the implications of this perspective in the midst of international conflicts, political battles, and culture wars? How do our praises enhance God's reputation and our own?

7. How do the last few verses of Psalm 69 shape our view of the world? Who inherits God's blessings? How does that awareness shape our vision as we go through trying and troubling times?

SESSION 4: BOOK 3, PSALMS 73–89

1. Book 3 is a relatively short collection of psalms filled with trials and anguish. How do the ancient Israelites' responses to God in their crises help us with our responses to him in ours? What do these psalms show us about how God hears and responds to his people?

2. In what way is Psalm 77 a model for praising God when our hearts don't feel like it? How does it show us the benefits of shifting our focus from our problems to his goodness? What happens in our hearts when we make that shift?

3. In what ways is our faith intergenerational, as Psalm 78 (particularly verses 6-7) shows us? Why is it important for us to live with that focus? Why do you think inheritance is so valued by God?

4. What is the difference between seeking God (the One who shines, per Psalm 80) and seeking the things of God (the shining itself)? Why is it important to make that distinction in our hearts? What does it mean to seek his face, and what are the rewards of doing so?

5. Why is social justice, as described in Psalm 82, a Kingdom issue for believers rather than a political issue? Why is it important for those who seek God's Kingdom to address social ills? In what ways is the absence of shalom in our world a call to action, an invitation to do something?

6. Why is a single day in God's courts better than a thousand anywhere else (Psalm 84:10)? Do you think most Christians live as though this is true? Why or why not? If someone truly believed this, what would their life look like?

SESSION 5: BOOK 4, PSALMS 90–106

1. Book 4 presents numerous pictures of seasoned, mature faith. What kinds of experiences and responses bring our faith to that point? Why do you think trials strengthen the faith of some and weaken the faith of others?

2. What does it mean to "live in the big picture," the vision given to us by Psalm 93 and others? Why do we get caught up in the smaller details of life and miss the bigger story going on around us? What can we do to expand our vision and live in sync with what God is doing?

3. According to the commentary on Psalm 96, what is the difference between the gospel of salvation and the gospel of the Kingdom? How does a strong vision of the Kingdom change how we live?

4. How does Psalm 97 picture God's throne and his presence? What does this portrayal tell us about his nature? What can we do to align ourselves with the environment and energy of his throne room?

5. Does the soundtrack in your mind on most days sound anything like Psalm 100? Why or why not? How can we retrain our minds to be filled more consistently with gratitude and praise?

6. In what sense are God's people exhibit A in God's restoration project for this world? How can we demonstrate eternal realities, even as heaven and earth appear to "wear out like old clothing" (Psalm 102:26)? How does God's restoration of Israel from captivity serve as a prophetic image of his plans for the earth?

7. How does David talk himself into truth in Psalm 103? Why do we sometimes need to convince ourselves of God's extravagant promises? How can we cultivate stronger faith in them?

SESSION 6: BOOK 5, PSALMS 107–150

1. Book 5 of Psalms emphasizes a renewed vision—hope after hard times, restoration on top of redemption. In what ways does Israel's history represent the story of the gospel?

2. Why is it important to know that the King not only rules "over" his enemies (Psalm 110:2) but also "in the midst" of them (see NKJV)? How might that change how we approach our spiritual battles?

3. Many psalms, like Psalm 111, give us hints and images of a global mission. Why is it vital for believers to live with a worldwide vision? How are God's people one of the ways his glory covers the earth?

4. In what sense is each believer a rags-to-riches story, as Psalm 113 describes? Why is it important to remember both where we came from and how high God has raised us?

5. What is the difference between reading God's Word as an instruction manual and immersing ourselves in its truths to the point that we embody and exude them? How does Psalm 119 express his Word's role in our lives?

6. Do you tend to see God as a passive observer or as someone who is on your side, as Psalm 124:1 says? How do our lives change when we realize how thoroughly he supports, sustains, and advocates for us?

7. In what sense is our faith a corporate gift to be experienced in fellowship? Why do you think our fellowship as believers is so pleasing to God (see Psalm 133)?

8. What do our "anxious thoughts" (Psalm 139:23) say about our view of God? How can an awareness of his presence reorient our thoughts and give us peace?

9. Why do you think it's significant that the last five psalms begin and end with "Praise the Lord!"? What does this say about the role of praise in our lives?

About the Author

CHRIS TIEGREEN has touched the lives of millions of people through his twenty-seven books, forty-plus study and discussion guides, many magazine and newspaper articles, and joint projects with other communicators. He has authored nine One Year devotionals, and his curricular and collaborative works have been translated into more than sixty languages, reaching many countries around the world. His experience in media, ministry, and higher education brings a unique perspective to his writing, which ranges from biblical teaching and devotional themes to cultural and historical commentary. Chris and his wife live in Atlanta.

NOTES